The Routledge Guide to Teaching Translation and Interpreting Online

Routledge Guides to Teaching Translation and Interpreting is a series of practical guides to key areas of translation and interpreting for instructors, lecturers, and course designers.

The Routledge Guide to Teaching Translation and Interpreting Online is for educators of translation and interpreting teaching online in a variety of curricular combinations: fully online, partially online, hybrid, multimodal, or face-to-face with online components. Offering suggestions for the development of curriculum and course design in addition to online tools that can be used in skill-building activities, and adaptable to specific instructional needs, this textbook is suitable for both multilingual and language-specific classes.

Fully comprehensive, the book addresses the tenets and importance of process-oriented pedagogy for students of translation and interpreting, best practices in online curriculum and course design, instructor online presence, detailed illustrations of specific online assignments, the importance of regular and timely feedback, and teaching across the online translation and interpreting (T&I) curriculum.

Written by two experienced translators, interpreters, and scholars who have been teaching online for many years and in various settings, this book is an essential guide for all instructors of translation and interpreting as professional activities and academic disciplines.

Cristiano Mazzei holds an MA in translation studies from the University of Massachusetts Amherst, USA, and is currently Director of Online Education for the College of Humanities and Fine Arts at the same institution. In addition to being certified as a translator and interpreter by different organizations in Brazil and the United States, Mazzei has vast experience teaching and training in both workshop and university settings.

Laurence Jay-Rayon Ibrahim Aibo holds a PhD in translation studies from the Université de Montréal, Canada. She has been translating, teaching, and interpreting in the Americas, Europe, and Africa for the past 30 years. She currently teaches in the online Certificate in Professional T&I program at the University of Massachusetts Amherst, USA, and is the author of *The Politics of Translating Sound Motifs in African Fiction* (2020).

Routledge Guides to Teaching Translation and Interpreting
Series Editor: Kelly Washbourne

Routledge Guides to Teaching Translation and Interpreting is a series of practical guides to key areas of translation and interpreting for instructors, lecturers and course designers. Drawing on authors' expertise and experience and on documented practice from the literature of the field, the guides include: an overview of critical concepts and approaches; sample tasks and activities; instructor notes; lesson plans and teaching resources; discussion prompts for key reading; and a glossary of terms. Authoritative and accessible, the guides present models of best practice in creative and intentional teaching and learning.

The Routledge Guide to Teaching Translation and Interpreting Online
Cristiano Mazzei and Laurence Jay-Rayon Ibrahim Aibo

For more information on any of these and other titles, or to order, please go to www.routledge.com/Routledge-Guides-to-Teaching-Translation-and-Interpreting/book-series/RGTTI

The Routledge Guide to Teaching Translation and Interpreting Online

Cristiano Mazzei and
Laurence Jay-Rayon Ibrahim Aibo

LONDON AND NEW YORK

Cover image: © Getty Images

First published 2022
by Routledge
2 Park Square, Milton Park, Abingdon, Oxon OX14 4RN

and by Routledge
605 Third Avenue, New York, NY 10158

Routledge is an imprint of the Taylor & Francis Group, an informa business

© 2022 Cristiano Mazzei and Laurence Jay-Rayon Ibrahim Aibo

The right of Cristiano Mazzei and Laurence Jay-Rayon Ibrahim Aibo to be identified as authors of this work has been asserted in accordance with sections 77 and 78 of the Copyright, Designs and Patents Act 1988.

All rights reserved. No part of this book may be reprinted or reproduced or utilised in any form or by any electronic, mechanical, or other means, now known or hereafter invented, including photocopying and recording, or in any information storage or retrieval system, without permission in writing from the publishers.

Trademark notice: Product or corporate names may be trademarks or registered trademarks, and are used only for identification and explanation without intent to infringe.

British Library Cataloguing-in-Publication Data
A catalogue record for this book is available from the British Library

Library of Congress Cataloging-in-Publication Data
A catalog record for this book has been requested

ISBN: 978-0-367-71105-4 (hbk)
ISBN: 978-0-367-71103-0 (pbk)
ISBN: 978-1-003-14931-6 (ebk)

DOI: 10.4324/9781003149316

Typeset in Sabon
by Apex CoVantage, LLC

Contents

Introduction   1
KELLY WASHBOURNE

1 Online Translation and Interpreting Education   14
   1.1 *Distance Learning and Translation and Interpreting (T&I)* 14
   1.2 *Multilingual vs. Language-Specific T&I Education* 16
   1.3 *Technology Literacy* 17
   1.4 *Culturally Responsive Pedagogy* 19
   1.5 *Universal Design for Learning (UDL)* 20
   1.6 *Online Student Engagement* 21
      1.6.1 *Synchronous* 22
      1.6.2 *Asynchronous* 23
      1.6.3 *Challenges with Regard to Engagement* 23
   1.7 *Does Online Teaching Make Us Better Teachers?* 24
   1.8 *The Time-Consuming Development Phase* 25
   1.9 *The Role of Artificial Intelligence (AI) in Online Courses* 25

2 Process-Oriented and Skill-Building Pedagogy   30
   2.1 *Translation* 30
   2.2 *Interpreting* 31
   2.3 *Self-Regulated Students* 32
   2.4 *Reflective Practice* 34
   2.5 *Reflections on the Translation Process* 34
      2.5.1 *Translation Process Steps* 35
      2.5.2 *Translation Process Reflection* 36
   2.6 *Reflective Practice in Interpreting* 41
   2.7 *Multilingual T&I Classes* 42
   2.8 *T&I Teaching Materials for Multilingual Classes* 44

3	**Online Course Development**	47

    3.1 *Practices and Tools* 48
        3.1.1 *Learning Stations or Safe Practice Spaces* 48
        3.1.2 *Self-Reflections* 48
        3.1.3 *Self-Evaluations* 48
        3.1.4 *Selection of Readings* 49
    3.2 *Writing a Syllabus* 49
        3.2.1 *Why Should We Write Detailed Syllabi?* 50
        3.2.2 *Why Should We Repeat Instructions in Different Places?* 52
        3.2.3 *Should We Give Syllabus Quizzes?* 52
        3.2.4 *Should We Use Screenshots?* 53
    3.3 *Designing Learning Outcomes* 54
    3.4 *Selecting an LMS* 55
    3.5 *Building Other Digital Tools into the Course Design* 58
        3.5.1 *Video Capture* 58
        3.5.2 *Sample Uses of Video Capture Technologies in the Online T&I Classroom* 60
        3.5.3 *VoiceThread* 60
        3.5.4 *Padlet* 61
        3.5.5 *Quizlet* 61
        3.5.6 *Discord* 61

4	**Instructor Presence in Online Courses: Synchronous and Asynchronous Considerations**	63

    4.1 *How Can Instructors Address the Range of Digital Literacies Among Students?* 64
    4.2 *How Do Instructors Create and Maintain Online Presence in their Courses?* 67
    4.3 *What is the Role of Pre-Recorded Videos?* 71
        4.3.1 *Lecture Videos* 72
        4.3.2 *Tutorial Videos (Screencasting)* 75
        4.3.3 *Presence Videos* 75
    4.4 *Instructor and Peer Feedback* 76
    4.5 *A Few Words About the Do's and Don'ts of Communication in Online Courses* 82

5	**Assessments, Rubrics, and Assignments**	85

    5.1 *Theory in Translator and Interpreter Training* 85
    5.2 *Assessment* 86
    5.3 *Learning Objectives and Outcomes* 87

5.4 Rubrics 89
5.5 Assignments 92
    5.5.1 Theoretical Discussions 92
    5.5.2 Translation of Texts 95
    5.5.3 Interpretation of Pre-Recorded Audio or Video Files 97
    5.5.4 Subtitling Exercises 101
    5.5.5 Live/Synchronous Interpreting Exams 103
5.6 Language Reviewers for Multilingual Translation & Interpreting Courses 111
    5.6.1 Who Are They? 112

6 Ethics in Online Translation and Interpreting Courses   115
6.1 The Impact of the Work of Translators and Interpreters on the Lives of Other People 116
6.2 Statuses and Livelihood of Translators and Interpreters Around the World: How are those Impacted by Changes in the Global Economy? 120
6.3 Ethical Implications of Machine Translation 122
6.4 Finding Practice Spaces Outside of Class 125
    6.4.1 Community Engagement and Service Learning 125
    6.4.2 Pre-Professional Collaborations Within and Across Institutions 129
6.5 Of Race, Privilege, Power Dynamics, and (In)Visibility 131
6.6 Sample Assignments in the T&I Ethics Classroom 134
    6.6.1 Translation Assignment 134
    6.6.2 Interpretation Assignment 135
6.7 Other Assignments for the Online Ethics Classroom 136

7 Conclusion: Final Considerations   143

Index   150

Introduction

Kelly Washbourne

Michel Serres tells us in *The Troubadour of Knowledge* (2006) that learning involves painful yet thrilling encounters with otherness; he likens the learner to the swimmer who departs from home, from the familiar, risking a voyage to the strange horizon. Education occurs in the fluid middle, in the crossing, the no-longer-at-home-not-yet-quite-arriving. And Ronald Barnett, in *A Will to Learn: Being a Student in an Age of Uncertainty* (2007) likens the student to the jumper, a ritual land diver from the N'gol in the South Pacific who, vines mooring his ankles amid the trees, launches himself into pure unknowingness and trust, the void the only medium in which "a new phase of human being" is made possible.

Are we to make so bold as to imagine translation and interpreting (T&I) teaching and learning as such radical change and risk, as transformation of being as well as knowing? *And why not?* Amid the pursuit of skills, it has been easy to forget that learning involves a change of perspective, of attitude, of *self*. Breakthroughs in understanding neuroplasticity tell us that the learner even changes *physically*. An ontological turn in education has been under way, though its rumblings have reached our field only faintly. Dall'Albaa and Barnacle describe it as a shift from what students acquire to who students become, or as "the embodiment of knowledge, or knowing" (2007, 681). Skills are indispensable, but let us see them endure, placed in the service of *habits of mind* and *ways of being in the world*. The model poses a direct challenge to skill-building as our only purpose as educators; we go wrong not in skillification but in the fact that "knowledge and skills are seen as attributes that can be decontextualised from the practices to which they relate" (ibid., 680). Situated learning has gained ground as a foundational model of the movement from noviceship to expertise, skopos, or purpose, has dethroned equivalent meanings and installed what a text *does*, and translator sociology and translator psychology now open windows into who is behind the *doing* and to whom the doing is done. And the pendulum of education in translation and interpreting is moving toward *how to be a translator or interpreter*, and away from merely *how to translate or interpret*. Metastudies (e.g. Xiu Yan, Jun Pan, and Wang 2015) have revealed that we largely reduce teaching and learning to content.

DOI: 10.4324/9781003149316-1

We diminish our task by focusing largely on *what to learn* and even miss the bigger picture by expanding our care to *how to teach it*; we bypass *who is learning* and *why*, and who is teaching and why. "Teach students, not subjects" is no mere slogan.

The great problem of learning is that of transfer, applying what is learned to novel environments and avoiding what the philosopher Alfred North Whitehead (1929) called *inert knowledge*, knowledge not activated when it is relevant in a context different from that of initial learning; it is knowledge that cannot be built upon or recombined. Two models toward promoting transfer have been used in online learning fruitfully, although we could mention far more. The first is anchored instruction, an approach whereby students research to engage with a problem through a narrativized macro-context and apply concepts to a new problem domain. In this book you will see examples and opportunities for these components, such as the cross-cultural comparison of ethical standards in the field. The second is absorb-do-connect, a model designed by William Horton (2012). In the first phase, the learner focuses on accretion (new knowledge) or restructuring previous knowledge, often through reading or watching; in the second, the knowledge is proceduralized in an activity, during which the student analyzes, verifies, debates, and applies; in the third, students extract the relevance of the task to their own lives. John Dewey advised that students be given "something to do, not something to learn" and that "the doing is of such a nature as to demand thinking or the intentional noting of connections" (1916, 181), and we might say that an efficient "nature" is pitched at the right level, supported by scaffolding, and designed with germane cognitive load. The beauty and the simplicity of the absorb-do-connect model is that one can *start* with the students' own lives, whether as activists or allies, volunteers, or in many service capacities such as paralegals, outreach support workers, interns at a hospital, student teachers, refugee liaisons, or representatives of job and family services. Our field is positioned now not only to lead global learning (whatever that might mean for different higher education institutions) but also to develop civic competence, that is, for supporting local as well as international changemaking.

When we connect and foster connection—the visual motif of this book's cover—we are engaging authentically. Authenticity in the classroom has been theorized about for every known part of the educational context. Shaffer and Resnick (1999) nearly a generation ago defined authenticity as multipartite: "real-world authenticity, assessment authenticity, disciplinary authenticity, and personal authenticity," integrated into a cluster concept they called *thick authenticity* (Skov Fougt et al. 2019, 479). These types, in order, are activities connected to the world at large (that is, they are not contrived, pedagogical tasks), and must have consequences to motivate performance. Assessment tasks should be like the tasks students perform while learning; students must think as they do in the discipline, sharing experts' tools, methods, and values, and the learning must be personally meaningful (ibid., 481–2). The tensions and contradictions are clear: How can one create coherence, or true authenticity? Their solution, thick authenticity,

> refers to activities that are personally meaningful, connected to important and interesting aspects of the world beyond the classroom, grounded in a systematic approach to thinking about problems and issues, and which provide for evaluation that is meaningfully related to the topics and methods being studied.
>
> (Shaffer and Resnick, 203)

If Anthony Pym (2009, 31–44), musing on the humanization of translation history, is right that the translator is a valid object of inquiry, and is an organizing principle as valid as texts and contexts, it stands to reason that the classroom can be the first place for studying and self-studying the protagonistic role of translators, as it is here that their discursive presence in histories and microhistories, their allegiances, their interculturalities, and the development of their identities, takes place. If the heroic translators are objects of knowledge, the everyday ones, including students, can be as well, even if the black box of their minds is just as partially accessible. We are witnessing a historical moment in academia in which the humanization of translation studies and the honoring of student subjectivities in education are in convergence. Translation as a factory model of inputs and outputs, and teaching as stimulus and response, are receding to make educational room for translation as a dialogic, human-centric, complex, embodied, purposeful, decision-making activity. If we revisit Chesterman's eight phases of translation, ages which he tell us are those of the translator also, we see a progression from a conception of translation as copying or imitating to more modern ideas of the translator as recoding, communicating, manipulating, and thinking. He suggests that a future phase may be *translating is rendering value judgments* (2016, 48), though there are signs that this era is already upon us. Interpreters, similarly, coordinate dialogue, assess and repair communication breakdowns, and exhibit empathy and emotional intelligence strategically, rather than serving as mechanistic witnesses to events. The evolution of translation and interpreting also parallels Blooms' taxonomy (see Chapters 3 and 5 herein) from bottom to top: In the beginning, a highly mimetic, imitative, fetishizing of the source; in time, expansive, interpretive, target-oriented, and creative; this is the progression from lower order thinking to higher. (Of course, this evolution model flatters us as evolved, but beware, all mapmakers place themselves at the center. And as in Bloom, the lower orders are not necessarily lower, nor are they dispensable, or even discrete stages, necessarily. In T&I we may be thinking and evaluating but we are *also* copying—who would argue against the need for the practitioner's imitative faculty?)

Whether you are a new or an experienced teacher, flexibility and experimentation are the watchwords. Abandon a task sooner rather than staying faithful to one that is impeding the learning, or to busyness that is amusing but low-impact. Take notes immediately after a session on what went well and what could use tuning (or better, edit tasks *right then*). If an idea is mastered, change one variable, then two: Does that complicate the perception? Rectify gaps at the beginning of the next class (e.g., assign a 1-minute essay: *What is the haziest point from last session?*). If students are telling you in so many words that blogs have grown stale, try podcasts, role plays, mock conferences, or a trial. If the same students are always dominating an online plenary discussion, let them try hand-signals that indicate whether a given student wants to build on something said, or to disagree, or to confirm or disconfirm comprehension; deputize a person often left out but who has thoughtful input to lead discussion. Invite a colleague to sit in on a session, or to serve as a sounding board. Or record the session for feedback (record it anyway, as increasingly this is part of a teaching portfolio) and do the hard work of self-reflection by checking your ego a moment: What tics do you have as a facilitator? Is the "hang time" too short or long when questions are asked? Are you the only one asking questions? Are there exclusions of student points of view or of disciplinary perspectives you didn't realize (or which are not given a fair hearing)? Are there logical transitions, thematic connections, and graduated difficulty between tasks? Are there opportunities for students to do post-mortems on activities? On the level of curriculum, is a course no longer responsive to community, industry, or government needs? Have you thought of cross-curricular teaching or a consortium? Could a virtual job fair be organized? And so on.

As compelling as our swimmer and diver are as metaphors of learning, in trying times especially, we must account for the social aspect of learning. George Herbert Mead wrote memorably that the student "does not become social by learning [but] must be social in order to learn" (1964 [1910], 122). Educationalists consider students today, especially online, as part of communities of practice, actor-networks, or even through the poststructuralist lens of rhizomatic learning: the metaphor and methodology of a centerless, boundless, unstructured structure made of nodes that can grow and spread and react to changing task conditions, and where "the community is the curriculum" (Cormier 2008).

Many strategies for learning online are richly social. To name a few:

- online artifact jigsaw
- student-determined assignment (involving student choice)
- student moderation assignment
- webinar or virtual conference
- writing an article for publication or presenting a poster
(Thormann and Kaftal Zimmerman 2012)

Online learning does not mean students have to become anonymous, or for that matter, that the teacher should surveil and weigh every move students make just because they can. Participation can and should take different forms, and vocally reticent students may prefer to write their contributions (although, of course, we do not favor only those forms of proficiency in which students are already comfortable). The student translator or interpreter tests their social limits with kinds of presence or personae. We can think of the T&I student's identity in Clifford's (1988, 29) terms: Identity is not a border but a subject's nexus of interactions. A translator or interpreter, and a learner, *are* within webbed relations; the dialogue, trialogue, or polylogue of their immediate online community; as well as the imagined communities of other learners worldwide and professionals in the field. The "multiple voices of the translation classroom," in González-Davies' (2004) turn of phrase, means that the classroom is a *text*, a weaving. The individual translator is even textualized as a multiplicity. Colombian scholar Martha Pulido (2016, 244) characterizes the translator as an explicit textual presence, a "site of exchange" (following Betty Bednarski [1999, 127]); for Pulido the translator is a reader who opens a space of hospitality.

In 1961, Emmanuel Levinas wrote *Totality and Infinity*. Its application to pedagogy is striking: He advocates the imperative to respond to the call of the Other by allowing choice and empowerment, and recognizing what he calls the Infinite in the student. When students are infinite, they are beyond the ability to be totalized. In some ways teaching ethically begins with acknowledging the unknowability of the Other and yet valuing meaningful encounters with them; our pedagogies must curricularize all manner of meaningful encounters. Guoping Zhao writes:

> While totalitarianism is the movement of reducing the other to the same either by eliminating or by absorbing the other, the philosophy of difference attempts to show the very irreducibility of otherness and the very impossibility of total sameness and presence.
>
> (Zhao 2016, 323)

The author, following Levinas, also notes:

> '[Teaching] designates an interior being that is capable of a relation with the exterior, and does not take its own interiority for the totality of being' (Levinas 2013 [1969], 180). Teaching and learning are about encountering the new and strange, about being interrupted and called into responsibility to the Other.
>
> (ibid., 324)

This says much about dialogue: Dialogue recognizes our humility, and our openness to being "interrupted" into strangeness; estrangement through dialogics is, not coincidentally, the path of translation. If a translation is a dialogue of many kinds, so too is teaching. Aloni neatly sums up the kinds of dialogue that have predominated in educational tradition:

(a) The **Socratic** dialogue, which is intellectually empowering in that it does not offer regurgitated knowledge and ready-made answers but creates discomfort concerning a given issue or dilemma and guides the student in a process of self-discovery and critical reasoning with a constant feeling of being "on the way."
(b) The **Nietzschean** dialogue, which empowers the student's autonomy and authenticity by rejecting the option of mass conformity and encourages the alternative of building the students' selfhood based on self-definition and self-creation.
(c) The **Buberian** dialogue, which develops a caring and empathetic sensitivity in interpersonal relationships by substituting professional and hierarchic alienation with sincere and attentive encounters, in which both the teacher's and the student's personality are completely present.
(d) The **Rogersian** dialogue, which enhances the individual's faith in one's ability to lead a successful life by tuning in and getting to know oneself.
(e) The **Freireian** dialogue, which helps students from weak and oppressed social groups to free themselves of inhibitory and regressive forces through the development of active knowledge and critical literacy and their application in a political struggle for social justice and equal opportunities.
(f) The **ecological** dialogue, reinforcing empathy for one's natural environment.

(2011, 43)

What kind of virtual classroom elicits learning-conducive dialogue for transformation? As science is a collective enterprise, consider the conceit of *classroom as laboratory*. The laboratory prizes newness; students are not working for the predetermined answer you expect, but from genuine inquiry toward discovery. Three microcases follow. For instance, conduct an experiment: One group reads the theoretical reading in the source text, another in translation, and then they discuss it—do they realize they are discussing different texts? Where are the disjunctures and interpretive divergences? Second, how important is reading translations of texts translated *out of* one's mother tongue for renewing one's perspective of the text? Take an article or a creative work that is familiar to the group; consider it now in translation. What readings did the translator give the text that perhaps the group missed, what textures emerged that only translation could unearth? (Are your students not doing the assigned readings? Assign the next theoretical reading *as the translation assignment*.) Now, third, interpreting: Everyone knows about translationese, but do students know there is an interpretese? And does their knowledge of it go beyond having simply been told of it? Why take researchers' word for it? Students can devise a way to work together to test the hypothesis, perhaps using some exploratory reception data, or they can see what characteristics emerge in contradistinction to translationese for a given language pair. Or the group can work on a rubric together to decide if or how the concept should be part of meaningful feedback for interpreting learners—does interpretese impede interpreting quality? How do you know for sure? Testing and ranking can be performed on ideas, tools, quality, processes, and more. Consider researching a phenomenon that has gained visibility in the field. For instance, is legalese becoming less formal and less given to compounds such as "hereinbefore" and archaisms such as "witnesseth" in favor of plain language? How can the sea change be verified objectively (e.g., a corpus)? If true, how should this affect the translator's construction of a brief and their decision-making about register, and does the shift affect the rigor of legal drafting? Or, a colleague recently claimed that clients care only for speed now, not quality, and that unedited machine translation (MT) is going out onto customer-facing pages to no complaints. A provocative prompt if there ever was one! Is this trend actually happening to a great extent, and if so, what does it portend? *Why* would it be happening? Hold that thought—grab your students and get to the lab and find out.

Your course may even literally designated a "lab!" That is no scientific bias, but a metaphor we can live by: There, students are researchers into authentic problems, they conduct controlled experimentation, and engage in collaboration and discovery learning in a technologized environment. (Translations and interpretations are experiments, as learners are their own "human experiments!") Discovery in such environments depends much on letting students determine the problem domain, rather than setting out the problem and solution path for them. In this connection, the analog world has used procedures that now are transforming. Consider *multilingual e-discovery*, the triaging and classifying of documents for translation for submission to the court. How can one replicate or simulate these efficiencies in the brave new digital world? Part of the rewards of teaching online is overcoming this kind of challenge, for it offers the designer, instructor, and students opportunities to teach and learn in ways that have not quite been tried before.

In these few pages, we have already made the comparison between translation, interpreting, and education. Basamalah's meditation (2020) on education as formation, as an enlargement through "translational elaboration," even extends to education as mutual transformation, with *the teacher transforming as well* in order to be accessible to learners.

Value-Addedness, User-Centeredness

Given the "rise of the machines" as a perceived threat in many quarters, T&I education can focus on what is irreplaceably human about our skillset: "translators will be in demand in those areas where human translation provides clients with the added value of intuition, creativity, ethical judgment and adaptability" (Massey 2017). Massey argues that

> [t]ranslators must be educated to develop, and above all maintain, the adaptive expertise needed to cope with the idiosyncratic, ill-defined problems that translation necessarily involves (Muñoz Martín 2014, 9), which are especially prevalent in those segments where value-adding human translation will be increasingly called for.[1]

That is, we do well to emphasize the human part of human translation: "translation as an adaptive, (co-creative, mediatory and advisory activity)." In part, Massey posits interaction with translation stakeholders as a pressing need in this connection, and thus interpersonal competence is an indispensable learning outcome. Massey and Ehrensberger-Dow (2017, 308–9), with an eye to the empathic competence needed for the production of any persuasive texts, "propose a stronger focus on user-centered multilingual text production and the development of writing, adaptation and transcreational skills, supplemented by a solid grounding in marketing, PR, branding, intercultural mediation and the cognitive semantics that underlie conceptual blending and transfer" (see also *User-Centered Translation* by Suojanen, Koskinen, and Tuominen 2014).

This First Edition

The text you are reading builds from the "why," through the "what" and the "how," and keeps in mind, always, the "who." Each iteration, each classroom, will be inimitable. Modular, customizable, inclusive, culturally sensitive, and contemporary, this Routledge Guide, the first in the new series, can accompany the emerging and seasoned educator alike, at all levels and in all environments of T&I training and education, and support all phases of the learning, from planning to course and curricular revision. The authors' experience often serves as a starting point and is built upon with research-based insights and best practices from self-reflective careers, including from the administrative perspective. This text promises to be the first of what I hope are many editions; a text to launch ideas, test out, build upon, personalize, and grow with as it too expands and updates.

In my seminar on translation pedagogy, I am sometimes told by my doctoral students from around the world who have come to our program in Kent, OH, United States: "The progressive teaching ideas we learn with you are most interesting, Professor, but in my country, for instance, a teacher would be fired if he admitted he didn't know something. Professors are expected to lecture, and to have all the answers."

To which on a good day I might say something like, "Saving face is an important practice in comparatist cross-cultural pedagogics, but does pretending to know accord with the science of teaching and learning? The

Socratic paradox is one's knowledge of knowing nothing, and the finding of wisdom in that. But we needn't be literalists—of *course* teachers may know many things, but the point is, teaching isn't a form of charismatic contagion, and *telling* isn't teaching, but anti-learning. Teaching is setting up conditions, opportunities for learning to take root organically. As for importing modern ideas of teaching and learning around the world, no one is calling for an overthrow of anything overnight, simply for the idea to be considered that *teachers, like translators, can accept or challenge norms of the field*. You can lecture in ways that are highly participatory (search for "modified lecture," for instance). You can foster responsibility for learning without abdicating authority. And instead of saying, "I don't know" to a question, say, "Let's find out together," and leave what *you* know out of it—an awful lot of teaching is just getting out of your students' way. And here's the important part: *Tell the students what you are doing, and why*; liberational teaching methods require student accomplices, regardless of country, and sometimes the doors themselves are removed from the jambs, and still students may stay encaged in their tentativeness until they are acclimated again to the freedom in which they were born."

A few summers ago, I found myself working with a non-governmental organization (NGO) on a coffee plantation deep in the Guatemalan jungle. One of our group's projects was setting up photovoltaic cells for electricity in order to build a cyberschool and library for the children of the local coffee workers. Sharing a repertoire of American games with the children, and theirs with us, was illuminating and good fun, until at one point, perhaps fancying myself the Marco Polo of sports diplomacy, I gathered them around in the clearing and said, "Kids, now we're going to learn dodge ball." All was explained procedurally and strategically, and transadapted linguistically. But at the moment of choosing a player from the opposing team to strike with the ball, their lively play from before now turned to inert sheepishness; they stopped all play and stared vacantly, neither refusing nor engaging, and silently. What was going on? Only gradually did it dawn on me that this was a highly collectivist culture and dodge ball involves *singling out* and *losing face*, two features of all-too-American competitive practices. Even in play, members of this rainforest community couldn't dishonor friends or family through an arbitrary punishment like hurling a ball at them; they rejected the means and thus the end of the game. For the game to survive in the jungle, I knew that either they would have to change or the game would—so, doubting either eventuality, I panicked and changed the game seamlessly to Crack the Whip, an inoffensive coordination game from pastoral times. I realized the limits of my own teaching perspective in that moment (and dodge ball's mercenary stupidity and cultural constructedness). In my epistemological bias (and ontological negligence), I had assumed *games always worked like games*, always self-identical, timeless, and placeless. And I realized that poor tasks are poor for various reasons (e.g., timing, execution, and set-up), like poor translations, but the poorest task is *any task for the wrong audience*. "What works" in education depends on the setting, and on the students, not on the universal applicability of a given design or approach. There is an instructional action, a skopos, just as there is a translatorial action. The skopos of the classroom is a living thing, ever-changing, "a map that is always detachable, connectible, reversible, modifiable, and has multiple entryways and exits and its own lines of flight" (Deleuze and Guatarri 1987, 21).

I will end this introduction with some axioms to bear in mind as you design and teach that may have different resonances for each reader, according to one's beliefs and experience, but that are a starting point for the voyage into the chapters ahead:

- A learning-centered classroom does not merely *re*produce knowledge; it *produces* knowledge and knowing.
- A learning-centered classroom looks chaotic from the outside; it always involves negotiations and improvisations, which are messy, non-linear, and inarticulate.
- Learning is first and last about learning to learn.
- Learning occurs from all sources.
- Learning is not only cognitive but emotional.
- Learning is accelerated by the act of teaching others, including from peer to peer.
- Learning depends on the conscious or unconscious disposition to learn.
- Learning, because it allows us to take part in fuller humanity than our own mind, is an alliance like translator-writer-reader or interpreter-interlocutors.
- Learning is no guarantee that today's solutions are tomorrow's panaceas; learning is provisional and partial.
- Learning is fed by challenge-seeking behavior.
- Learning, like an uncluttered room or mind or artistic composition, often is more alive the less it is laden with inputs, activity, and demands. Good learning, like a ripple on a watery surface, often expands powerfully into (and beyond) its confined space and time.
- Learning cannot only be routine but also must be resourceful and creative.[2]
- Plan for learning, but not all learning is planned.
- Learning is not constrained to class meetings.
- Learning should be transformative, but students may show it more through incremental realizations and subtle behavioral changes, than through a grand, cinematic awakening.
- Learning will involve some resistance.
- Learning is, and looks, different in different learners.
- Learning and unlearning have to be intimately related.
- Learning arises from deliberate practice, targeted feedback, and repetition with variation, not only from teaching.

- Learning, sometimes, is from the unknown toward the unknown, rather than from the known toward the unknown.
- Learning has to be earned, or it is contraband; if it is passive, it will not belong to the learner.
- Learning requires self-reflection on learning.
- Learning is not a threat to expertise but the hallmark of the expert. Expertise is not a noun but a present continuous verb.
- Learning is the student's natural state, and what obscures it must be removed.
- Learning is lifelong and lifewide.
- Learning, however strong or struggling, invites support.

This book is all in the name of access and accessibility, as the authors conclude. In this, education once again is translation and interpreting's twin. The online modality can go a long way toward alleviating at least some of the "learning deserts" of the world, and toward bringing more potential practitioners into the fold. Can language mediation and education be used for ends that are not constructive? Of course, but let us seek to educate translators and interpreters for a positive contribution to the world, for commerce and the collective good both, which goes beyond jobs to employability, beyond a commodity to a service, beyond skills to being, and beyond individual learning to collaborative learning. Online learning is with us to stay, and we are joined by leaders in online translator and interpreter education, Laurence Jay-Rayon Ibrahim Aibo and Cristiano Mazzei, to help guide the way forward. Moments in one's academic career as a student may indeed feel like land diving or long-distance swimming, but buoyed by the best practices detailed here, we can promote a safe haven for risk-taking in which all learners, and all teachers, can succeed.

Notes

1 Ill-defined or ill-structured problems encourage multiple perspectives and solutions, call on metacognition, and feature information that is unavailable or conflicting, and may have multiple constraints. Scholars have found well-structured problems to be insufficiently complex to be reflective of problems found "in the wild."
2 Great jazz musicians "outwit their learned habits by putting themselves in unfamiliar musical situations demanding novel responses." Leadership (and by extension, teaching) is "creating space, sufficient support, and challenge so that people will be tempted to grow on their own. The goal is the opposite of conformity: a leader's job is to create the discrepancy and dissonance to trigger people to move away from habitual positions and repetitive patterns. I've come to think of this key leadership capacity as "provocative competence" (Barrett 2012, 139).

References

Aloni, Nimrod. "Humanistic Education: From Theory to Practice." *Education and Humanism: Linking Autonomy and Humanity*, edited by Wiel Veugelers. Sense,

2011, pp. 35–46, https://link.springer.com/content/pdf/10.1007/978-94-6091-577-2_3.pdf.

Barrett, Frank J. *Yes to the Mess: Surprising Leadership Lessons from Jazz.* Harvard Business Preview Press, 2012.

Barnett, Ronald. *A Will to Learn: Being a Student in an Age of Uncertainty.* Open University Press/McGraw-Hill Education, 2007.

Basamalah, Salah. "Education as Translation: Toward a Social Philosophy of Translation." *inTRAlinea*, vol. 22, 2020, pp. 1–7.

Bednarski, Betty. "La traduction comme lieu d'éxchange." *Échanges culturels entre les deux solitudes*, edited by Marie-Andrée- Beaudet. Presses de l'Université Laval, 1999, p. 127.

Chesterman, Andrew. *Memes of Translation: The Spread of Ideas in Translation Theory.* John Benjamins Publishing Company, 2016.

Clifford, James. *The Predicament of Culture: Twentieth-Century Ethnography, Literature, and Art.* Harvard University Press, 1988.

Cormier, Dave. "Rhizomatic Education: Community as Curriculum." *Innovate: Journal of Online Education*, vol. 4, no. 5, 2008, Article 2, https://nsuworks.nova.edu/innovate/vol4/iss5/2.

Dall'Albaa, Gloria, and Robyn Barnacle. "An Ontological Turn for Higher Education." *Studies in Higher Education*, vol. 32, no. 6, 2007, pp. 679–91, DOI: 10.1080/03075070701685130.

Dewey, John. *Democracy in Education: An Introduction to the Philosophy of Education.* The Macmillan Company, 1916.

Deleuze, Gilles, and Félix Guatarri. *A Thousand Plateaus: Capitalism and Schizophrenia.* University of Minnesota Press, 1987.

González-Davies, María. *Multiple Voices in the Translation Classroom: Activities, Tasks and Projects.* John Benjamins, 2004.

Horton, William K. *E-Learning by Design.* Pfeiffer, 2012.

Levinas, Emmanuel. *Totality and Infinity: An Essay on Exteriority.* Duquesne University Press, 2013 [1969].

Massey, Gary. "New Roles and Tasks for the Translation Profession: Educating Translators for the Digital Present and Future [paper]." Translation Services in the Digital World: A Sneak Peek into the (near) Future. DG TRAD Conference, Luxembourg, 16–17 Oct. Luxembourg: Directorate General for Translation, European Parliament, 2017 [2018], pp. 36–51, https://doi.org/10.2861/4803.

Massey, Gary, and Maureen Ehrensberger-Dow. "Machine Learning: Implications for Translator Education." *Lebende Sprachen*, vol. 62, no. 2, 2017, pp. 300–12.

Mead, George Herbert. "The Psychology of Social Consciousness Implied in Instruction." *Selected Writings: George Herbert Mead*, edited by A.J. Reck. Bobbs-Merrill, 1964 [1910], pp. 114–22.

Muñoz Martín. "Situating Translation Expertise. A Review with a Sketch of a Construct." *The Development of Translation Competence Theories and Methodologies from Psycholinguistics and Cognitive Science*, edited by John W. Schwieter and Aline Ferreira. Cambridge Scholars Publishing, 2014, pp. 2–56.

Pulido, Martha. "What Is a Translator?" *Trad Florianópolis*, vol. 36, no. 2, 2016, pp. 237–52.

Pym, Anthony. "Humanizing Translation History." *Hermes—Journal of Language and Communication Studies*, no. 42, 2009, pp. 23–48.

Serres, Michel. *The Troubadour of Knowledge*, translated by Sheila Faria Glaser and William Paulson. University of Michigan Press, 2006.
Shaffer, D.W., and M. Resnick. "'Thick' Authenticity: New Media and Authentic Learning." *Journal of Interactive Learning Research*, vol. 10, no. 2, 1999, pp. 195–215.
Skov Fougt, Simon, Morten Misfeldt, and David Williamson Shaffer. "Realistic Authenticity." *Journal of Interactive Learning Research*, vol. 30, no. 4, 2019, pp. 477–504.
Suojanen, Tytti, Kaisa Koskinen, and Tiina Tuominen. *User-Centered Translation*. Routledge, 2014.
Thormann, Joan, and Isa Kaftal Zimmerman. *The Complete Step-by-Step Guide to Designing and Teaching Online Courses*. Teachers College Press, 2012.
Whitehead, Alfred North. *The Aims of Education*. Macmillan, 1929.
Xiu Yan, Jackie, Yang Jun Pan, and Honghua Wang. "Studies on Translator and Interpreter Training: A Data-Driven Review of Journal Articles 2000–12." *The Interpreter and Translator Trainer*, vol. 9, no. 3, 2015, pp. 263–86.
Zhao, Guoping. "Introduction: Levinas and the Philosophy of Education." *Educational Philosophy and Theory*, vol. 48, no. 4, 2016, pp. 323–30, DOI: 10.1080/00131857.2015.1041007.

1 Online Translation and Interpreting Education

First, we want to acknowledge that this book was written during one of the worst health crises the world has ever experienced together, the COVID-19 pandemic. Like many others around the globe, our interactions with our family members, co-workers, friends, and loved ones changed dramatically toward a more virtual experience. Like many other areas of life, education has been affected in major ways, with levels of disruption never seen before. In general, most educational institutions were not prepared to transition to a fully online environment and the process evolved gradually, with instructional designers working in overdrive to provide support to teachers. We are not sure how this will influence online learning in the future, but one thing is certain: Those who had never considered teaching online "were forced" to do so, and now have a more informed idea of the demands and realities of this type of educational space. Some of those who pivoted to remote teaching decided to try to emulate their in-person classes by requiring students to attend synchronous meetings, simply did not have time to learn online education best practices, or did not want to since we were all told the pandemic was temporary and that eventually we would all go back to "normal." All of this has led to a certain level of frustration among students who had to transition to a different educational environment, and who have cited increased stress and negative consequences to their health and social lives. However, it is not clear that education alone is the cause of such negative experiences, since all aspects of our lives have been changed due to the forced isolation caused by the coronavirus pandemic. The fact is that there has been a tremendous increase in distance learning as a result of this health crisis and many of our colleagues, especially those who resisted this environment for a long time, were surprised by what instructors and students were able to successfully do online.

1.1 Distance Learning and Translation and Interpreting (T&I)

Like any other technological development, online education has been met with skepticism since its inception, initially framed as "distance learning" in

DOI: 10.4324/9781003149316-2

the late 1980s. It owes a lot to other forms of remote education that came before it, including correspondence programs offered by postal services and classes broadcast by public television and radio networks across the globe, fostering the idea that students could study from their homes at their own pace. Distance learning has also been hailed as a way to democratize knowledge and education and improve literacy rates among adult populations in certain countries, including Brazil, which has had government-funded educational programs broadcast via radio and television since the 1920s (Barros Filho 2018).

While the democratizing power of virtual learning cannot be underestimated, one needs to take into account the many challenges faced by online learners, including the lack of access and cost of reliable Internet connections, computers/devices, and technology literacy levels. For example, a recent article on online T&I education efforts in some African countries because of the COVID-19 pandemic illustrates the stark differences between the Global North and Global South when it comes to access. Afolabi and Oyetoyan conducted qualitative research with T&I students and educators in the Republic of Benin, Cameroon, Nigeria, Senegal, and Togo, to find out about their experience pivoting to virtual learning in 2020 and 2021. Even though the response rate was low (20 out of 150 individuals), the results revealed that the "transition to online teaching and learning has not been smooth, due to the economic challenges, insufficient technological infrastructure and skilled human resources" (2021, 327). Despite creative efforts from teachers and institutions, including using WhatsApp for group discussions, receiving/sending assignments, and voice-recorded feedback, students listed poor or no Internet connection, electricity problems, and costly data plans as some of the challenges faced (341).

Moreover, professional and personal issues faced by many non-traditional students who seek online education, including working full-time while studying, raising families, and delayed pursuit of their education, also add to the complexities experienced by distance learners. However, according to Flower Darby (2019), "these factors are the very reason many of our online students choose to take college classes online. They need a flexible option that accommodates their work and family obligations" (8), which are important considerations that should guide teachers and instructional designers when developing their courses. Nevertheless, online education has grown incredibly fast in the last few years. According to the report *Grade Increase: Tracking Distance Education in the United States*, "distance education enrollments increased for the fourteenth straight year, growing faster than they have for the past several years" (Seaman, Allen, & Seaman 2018, 3).

Unlike many other disciplines, translation and interpreting have been late in joining virtual and distant learning, despite the fact that written translation, for example, has been practiced with the support of personal computers and the Internet in robust ways since the 1990s, and that interpreting has been offered via telephone since the 1970s. One finds sporadic research papers published on online translation and interpreting teaching, with topics ranging from the challenges of such an environment, to the need for educational approaches to reflect current technological developments, different tools available such as blogs, various learning management systems, theoretical underpinnings and pedagogies, and synchronous and asynchronous modalities (Chen and Ko 2009; Azizinezhad and Hashemi 2011; Sachtleben 2015; Gorozhanov, Kosichenko, and Guseynova 2018; Bilić 2020; Perramon and Ugarte 2020).

1.2 Multilingual vs. Language-Specific T&I Education

Until recently, most online translation and interpreting courses have been offered in language-specific classrooms and contexts. However, with increased migration trends, different language policies adopted by various wealthy nations around the world, and the growth of the field of community translation and interpreting, the demand and need for multilingual courses has increased tremendously. In the United States, for instance, more than 20% of US residents (66.6 million) do not speak English as a primary language at home and this number has doubled since 1990 and tripled since 1980. Those languages include Khmer, Hmong, Laotian, Punjabi, Urdu, Haitian Creole, and Vietnamese (Esther 2018); not to mention emerging languages that are a result of different new immigration waves, such as is the case of the Karen people from Myanmar, or indigenous languages from Central America, such as Q'anjob'al, K'iché, or Mam, as reported by The New York Times in an article about the dire need for interpreters in the US court system (Reefer 2019).

Multilingual translation and interpreting courses have diverse student populations in terms of their educational backgrounds and life experiences. Some of them are recent or late immigrants, many of whom have bachelor's degrees from their countries of origin in different areas; some have not completed their formal education in their native countries and languages, having achieved their high school diploma or General Educational Development (GED) certification in the new host country. Many of them are native English speakers who have pursued second language training and education; some have had extensive formal education in the language, including a bachelor's or a master's degree; and some have lived abroad for different lengths of time through study abroad programs. Some students are heritage speakers of their families' languages, including Hmong, Spanish, Korean, Somali, Portuguese, Haitian Creole, Cape Verdean Creole, etc., with different levels of proficiency in their ancestors' native languages. Because of the fragmented status of translation/interpreting professionalization and education, many of them are working interpreters and translators who have little, some, or no formal translation and interpreter training. Some of them have attended short professional workshops (40 to 120 hours) designed to meet the growing demand for trained translators and interpreters in various countries, while some want to pursue further education.

1.3 Technology Literacy

If online learning literacy is already an issue for native English speakers pursuing education in a wealthy nation such as the United States, imagine being a recent immigrant seeking to add new credentials, or finding a new career path, coming from a developing nation with little or no access to the Internet. According to a press release from the United Nations Conference on Trade and Development (UNCTD), "Almost half the world's population remains offline and excluded from the benefits of digitalization" (2019). Therefore, online multilingual translation and interpreting programs must meet these challenges if they are to succeed. For courses and trainings that are connected to a technical or community college or university, administrators should work closely with their institutions' available online support teams to make sure students have access to much-needed assistance in their first encounter with virtual learning, which ranges from video or written tutorials to 24/7 helpdesks with staff trained to interact with students whose first language is not the primary one spoken in the new host country. In some instances, administrators need to seek help from non-profit organizations and sometimes attempt hybrid models to help students overcome the initial hurdles of learning in an online environment.

This was the case, for example, for a large group of Karen students enrolled in a community college program in the state of Minnesota. In 2016, the Karen Organization of Minnesota (KOM), which was created to help integrate the new wave of immigration of more than 9,000 Karen and other refugees from Myanmar, partnered with a large community college, Century College, and the Roseville Adult Learning Center to apply for a grant from the Minnesota Department of Employment and Economic Development. The goal was to train Karen translators and interpreters to meet the dire and increasing need for cultural and language mediators across the state as the new immigrants tried to access public services in their journey of settling in their new host country. The translation and interpreting courses were delivered online by the community college with additional in-person support from the Roseville Adult Learning Center. Once or twice a week, Karen students met in-person in classrooms at the KOM's office with instructors who helped them navigate the online learning environment. Thanks to the success of the multilingual program initiative, the organization invited speakers of other languages to join the classes, including Kinyarwanda, French, and Swahili (Karen Organization of Minnesota 2020). After taking one course with in-person assistance, students continued to pursue the additional online classes on their own.

Online faculty members also play a major role in facilitating access to their courses for students with technology literacy issues. Because many first-time online instructors have never taken an online class themselves before, one great way to walk in our students' shoes is to enroll in one. If cost is an issue, or funding is not available at their teaching institutions, there are many opportunities to take virtual classes for free through massive open online courses (MOOCs) and other open-source platforms, such as Coursera. At the same time, online faculty members should work closely with their institutions' online education staff and instructional designers to learn best teaching practices in the virtual environment.

Instructors should get to know their students well in their first week of classes and identify those who are not participating actively due to technology or online literacy issues, which can be done through various "introductory" exercises in online forums or other rich media platforms that allow students to participate via a written comment, audio file, video, or other type of media. Faculty members should make every effort to reach out to those who are not participating to find out if one of the reasons is their inability to navigate technological challenges. Those efforts might include, but are not limited to, email correspondence, telephone, and texting applications such as WhatsApp. However, faculty members should work closely with school administrators and program directors for additional assistance in terms of policies and student privacy laws in different countries. In the United States, for instance, where the Family Education Rights and Privacy Act (FERPA) regulates the relationship between students and educational institutions, texting apps such as WhatsApp clash with the required privacy protections. A student's telephone number is considered "personal information collected from students" and may not be disclosed by instructors. There might be a workaround, but teachers must communicate with their institutions to find out about alternative platforms or the possibility of students signing a waiver and allowing their numbers to be shared inside a specific classroom. Obviously, students can decide to share their personal contact information with classmates and instructors.

Some students with technology and online learning challenges will not always respond well to all different types of virtual resources available and might need to speak to a "real person" to solve their issues. That is when strong and robust institutional support is crucial. In the current online Certificate in Professional Translation and Interpreting at the University of Massachusetts (UMass) Amherst, for example, despite all guideline documents, written and video tutorials, webpages, and different types of information available through different channels to help students understand registration and enrollment processes, academic pathways to completing the program, language proficiency requirements, etc., many students still want to speak to a "real person" on the phone or via videoconference to clarify or simply to connect to a human being in their online education journey. Therefore, program directors, instructors, and administrators should consider the investments that must be made so that there is a system in place to still offer additional "brick-and-mortar" support to certain students, including advising. In the age of access and equity, if one is serious about serving all students equitably, structures need to be put in place to make sure all participants have an equitable experience in online learning. According to Mike Weiss, an expert in online adult education methodologies, one of the reasons for low completion rates in online education is that courses are not meeting students' expectations. He adds, "your students are disappointed because they registered with false ideas on what your course is like. Maybe they expected the lessons to cover a specific topic more or maybe they expected the format to be different" (Weiss 2019). This clearly speaks to the importance of clear communication and information to students, including individual advising for certain students.

1.4 Culturally Responsive Pedagogy

Because of the many reasons mentioned earlier regarding diverse groups of students, accessibility and equity are particularly important concepts in multilingual translation and interpreting courses, and should be guiding forces in the decisions that faculty and program directors make when developing curricula. According to a report by the Association of College and University Educators (ACUE) in the United States, "achieving equity requires that we teach with practices that embrace the diversity of our students' backgrounds. We must also thoughtfully review our instructional approaches to identify—and change—any unintended practices that might limit student expectations and achievements" (2020). One of the authors' first encounters with deeper discussions about diversity and inclusion in education took place through a 1-year fellowship promoted by one of the institutions they taught at called "Culturally Responsive Pedagogy," which was offered to faculty members as a response by the department of education of that state to address the achievement gap between Black and white students. The work was grounded in a theoretical approach to education first proposed by Gloria Ladson-Billings (1995) in her article "Toward a Theory of Culturally Relevant Pedagogy," based on her empirical research on the success of eight teachers in a "small predominantly African American, low-income elementary school district in Northern California" (471). Wanting to challenge "deficit paradigms," in regard to previous studies that focused on the failure of students of color or lack of success of schools in addressing achievement gaps between Black and white students, Ladson-Billings set out to find out what successful teachers were doing right in guiding their students of color toward successful paths.

Other scholars have taken the concept further, for example, H. Samy Alim and Django Paris (2017) in "What is Culturally Sustaining Pedagogy and Why Does it Matter?" argue that:

> for too long, scholarship on "access" and "equity" has centered implicitly or explicitly around the White-gaze-centered question: How can

"we" get "these" working-class kids of color to speak/write/be more like middle-class White ones (rather than critiquing the White gaze itself that sees, hears, and frames students of color in everywhichway as marginal and deficient)?

(3)

In multilingual translation and interpreting classes, issues of power and gaze come up all the time among students with diverse cultural backgrounds, especially when languages of power (i.e., English, French, Spanish, German, etc.) are combined with minority, emerging, or languages of lesser diffusion, for instance, in the case of Australia, Dari, Tamil, Hazaragi, Nepali, and Farsi/Persian (Hlavac 2016). The most obvious power differential that instructors and students are faced with includes access to resources such as reputable dictionaries, research, online glossaries, etc. for minoritized and languages of lesser diffusion. The less obvious ones are assumptions and attitudes toward translation and interpreting strategies as social practices.

1.5 Universal Design for Learning (UDL)

As part of the work toward equity, diversity, and inclusion, the concept of UDL has been proposed, which can be succinctly described as an approach to curriculum that minimizes barriers and maximizes learning for all students. Its origins can be traced back to the Universal Design (UD) movement of the 1990s, created by architects who wanted to make public buildings and city streets accessible. The concept found fertile ground in education, with pedagogues adopting UD "as a conceptual and philosophical foundation on which to build a model of teaching and learning that is inclusive, equitable, and guides the creation of accessible course materials" (18). Some of the main principles and questions that help guide instructors in the design of their online courses based on the inclusive design framework include:

- How do I make my course student-centered?
- Do I clarify the steps students need to follow in order to learn through my course?

When it comes to diverse students:

- How do I design my course with distinct learners in mind and provide multiple paths for learning and success?

Regarding communicating with students:

- Do I use inclusive language in my syllabus?
- Is my content culturally inclusive?

- Do I use resources other than white experts?
- Am I perpetuating cultural stereotypes in my translation and interpreting assignments?

As for accessibility:

- Is my course easy to navigate?
- Are there many options for encountering content?
- Are my links clear (hypertext)?

Such questions should illuminate the fact that what we include in our online courses reflects our values and conveys to students how we see them as learners and citizens in our classes. Particularly for multilingual translation and interpreting courses, instructors should consider if their course examples reflect a diverse society, ensure that they are using student-friendly language and guiding questions, and offer key resources. Regarding the issue of perpetuating the stereotypes mentioned previously, educators must be careful when selecting authentic materials or using textbooks for T&I assignments. In particular, interpreting practice role-plays like the following examples must be interrogated and challenged in class, or replaced altogether: limited English proficient (LEP) immigrants always portrayed as criminals and witnesses describing suspects they saw as "tall Black men" in legal settings; or a young Latino boy's dream in an educational dialogue being depicted as wanting to become a cashier at a fast-food chain after being praised for his math skills—as if he could not aspire to other things. Another important concept in this framework is including students as co-constructors of knowledge, which can be done by simply creating student surveys about course content and resources or taking it a step further by inviting students to participate in the creation of assignments, rubrics, and course content. For specific examples of how to apply UDL, see Chapters 2 and 5.

1.6 Online Student Engagement

What does an engaged student look like to instructors? How does one build a learning community in their courses? For instructors of in-person classes, engagement might simply mean that students are not falling asleep in the middle of their classes. It might also mean students are asking questions, participating, and contributing to the classroom dynamics. In the virtual environment, such types of interaction will look a bit different, for both synchronous and asynchronous instruction. Some online instructors will say that it translates into having "lively" discussion boards, submitting assignments on time, responding to feedback from teachers, etc. Others might say that engaged students are those who are able to take away something from an online training and apply it to the workplace; those who are connecting content and knowledge with their own experience; or those who do research before asking questions, citing references, etc. Therefore, engagement looks different to various teachers and across courses because people have diverse sets of goals. Even if instructors are teaching the same class, it might look different to each one of them.

In addition to the selection of course content, the way instructors structure their courses and the opportunities they provide for students to communicate (including the channels available) with each other and with the teacher will affect how everyone builds relationships and forms a learning community. Moreover, the way students get to know each other—not only as students but as human beings—is important for them to succeed and fully participate in the course. This speaks to the idea of "social presence," which involves "open communication, affective expression, and group cohesion," as proposed by the community of inquiry (CoI) framework, a social constructivist model of online and hybrid learning processes (Purdue Repository for Online Teaching and Learning 2020, 1). Such relationships take time to build and involve trust, communication, and creating spaces and opportunity. In both synchronous and asynchronous courses, one thing is certain: Engagement is having positive and frequent interactions with course content, peers, and instructors, who function as facilitators. Moreover, when engaging with content, students should be internalizing it, critically analyzing it, and then applying it somewhere, demonstrating that they are on a pathway to achieving mastery.

1.6.1 *Synchronous*

There are several tools and platforms available for live meetings with students that instructors can use to deliver content while inviting students to work on different assignments individually or as a group. Teleconferencing platforms have quickly become very resourceful tools with different features that foster engagement. Icebreakers in a synchronous meeting, for example, contribute to the human and affective connection discussed previously. Some suggestions include asking students to turn on their cameras and inviting them to demonstrate how they feel by making facial gestures or through body movement. Afterward, all other students are encouraged to mimic the same gestures and movements. Instructors can model the icebreaker by being the first to express how they feel and then urging students to mimic them. The ideas and possible use of icebreakers in videoconference meetings are numerous and easily found online. T&I instructors can, for example, ask students to express how they feel by uttering a short sentence in another language and then asking another student who shares the same language pair to interpret it into the pivot language of the class. Icebreakers can also be done using the chat function of many of the platforms, by asking students to type a quick response or use one of the emojis available to express their reaction to some prompt.

If instructors are delivering content live on video, some engaging activities include polling, chat, and external platforms such as Google Docs where students can work on projects or different activities. Moreover, breakout rooms in teleconferencing platforms such as Zoom work really well for translation and interpreting exercises in groups or pairs. Synchronous meetings also lend themselves extremely well to final interpreting exams, and to skills building practice in the growing field of remote interpreting (RI).

1.6.2 Asynchronous

For courses and activities that require students to engage with content or each other at different times, pre-recorded lectures work really well for introduction of content. There are many video/screen recording platforms available, including freeware (Screencast-O-Matic), which can be used to record lectures. Echo360 and other similar systems also currently allow instructors to insert quizzes into recorded content, thus increasing student engagement. Students can only move on to the next segment of the video after they have answered the question and received pre-set feedback from the instructor. VoiceThread, a rich media interaction tool (discussed further in Chapter 3), is also a very resourceful platform to introduce concepts and engage the class around different topics, with students and instructors being able to make comments using text, audio, video, and different types of media. The same tool can be used for online discussions of articles and for asynchronous translation and interpreting practice.

Another way to increase engagement in nonsynchronous courses is to offer optional live meetings, which can include office hours, guest speakers, Q&As, etc. If not required, such encounters should be recorded and made available to students who were not able to attend due to emergencies, time difference, illnesses, or any personal or professional commitments.

1.6.3 Challenges with Regard to Engagement

Some of the challenges instructors usually indicate include getting students to effectively work with each other, monitoring and reviewing asynchronous comments in discussion boards in large classes, having to repeat ideas and information multiple times, reaching out to students who are missing or not participating, etc. Some challenges, such as getting students to participate, can be addressed, for example, by making it a requirement. A solution to the challenge of giving feedback to discussion boards is not to respond to each and every single entry by students, but rather highlight some of the excellent comments or common themes discussed by students, thus inserting oneself in the conversation when needed. For additional engagement in a discussion forum (either traditional written ones or newer versions such as VoiceThread), instructors could add an introductory video, sharing information about themselves, expectations for the course, goals, etc., which, in turn, might motivate students to participate. Moreover, a good idea for such short video or textual insertions is for instructors to include some information about what students will be doing in the following module or unit, thus introducing the next topics and making connections that students do not usually make on their own.

Moreover, telling students why they are doing something is a very good strategy to engage them and to get them involved with their own learning. Whatever engaging elements instructors decide to use, they need to make sure activities are aligned with learning objectives and support learning goals (discussed further in Chapter 5). Another suggestion is to use a variety of tools—ideally located inside the learning management system (LMS)—to keep them engaged and interested, but not too many since long learning curves might cause frustration among the group. Finally, educators need to make sure technologies are equitable and accessible and think about alternatives in case something or some technology does not work.

1.7 Does Online Teaching Make Us Better Teachers?

The authors of this book want to turn now to something that is very personal as a result of their journey from teaching face-to-face in the beginning of their careers as instructors to moving to mostly online a few years later. In an article published in the *Chronicle of Higher Education* in 2019, Kevin Gannon recounts how teaching in the online environment has made him, and other faculty members, better teachers. "We've found that elements of online pedagogy not only help us become better instructors in a fully digital learning space, but better at the craft of teaching in general" (Gannon 2019). He focuses on three aspects in the article, namely improved course design and assessment, enhanced student engagement, and learning to explain things better to students. When teaching in the physical world, instructors assume a lot of things as self-evident, or as he points out, "it's on the syllabus!" The same thing has happened to us over time; teaching online has made us take a closer look at the courses that we still teach in-person and revisit our assumptions about many things we thought were very clear. "It wasn't until my foray into online teaching that I stopped assuming that students would 'get' the point behind my practices and started explaining the why," adds Gannon when challenging the way he used to do things in class simply because he had done them that way before for so long. He concludes that teaching online demands the type of critical reflective practice that can make us all better teachers.

Moreover, in the in-person environment, there are norms, rules, and behaviors that pertain to classroom education that all students are already familiarized with by the time they get to the university. For example, students expect that they can clarify and ask questions to the instructor after the class is over; they might be reminded of an assignment they had forgotten because they suddenly saw their professor in the hallway; or students may rely, to varying degrees, on their social networks with other classmates to guide them in understanding course content, instructions, etc. Such physical social interactions are no longer available in the virtual environment, or are available in different ways, making it crucial that instructors spend a considerable amount of time designing their online courses, testing their ideas, and coming up with plans B, C, and D in case some technical issue happens.

1.8 The Time-Consuming Development Phase

New faculty members embarking in online teaching should have an understanding about how much time goes into the development phase—a lot of times unpaid, sadly—and the importance of preparing for different kinds of scenarios. In terms of online course design, one of the things that has been helpful in the US context is to replicate one's syllabus in the LMS. Most faculty members at colleges and universities are very familiar with designing their own syllabi or using the syllabi of other professors and instructors, which are, in general, detailed documents about course delivery. Syllabi also serve a legal purpose in US higher education for situations when students and instructors have disagreements about course load and expectations. Overall, US syllabi are composed of six overarching areas: relationship with instructor (office hours, communications, etc.); course description and goals; content (textbook, articles, videos, different types of materials); learning outcomes; grading system (assessments, assignments, rubrics); university resources; and policies. This type of information is a good roadmap for instructors working on developing their remote classes, for example, if one has a clear idea of all the assignments students will be required to complete and when and how much they are worth in the grading scheme, the inclusion of those items in one's course shell will be much easier. Likewise, if all articles for reading assignments (discussion forums, VoiceThread, or other types of online discussion tools) are selected and scheduled clearly on one's syllabus, and how they will be made available in the course shell determined, the process of transferring those items to the LMS can be very seamless. One piece of advice here is to make those items available in different ways and places. For example, one can have all the articles compiled by the university's digital library resources in one major list accessed by a link (i.e., "Course Materials") but also make them accessible via different links under the weeks they are expected to be discussed, with clear metadata, including bibliographic information.

1.9 The Role of Artificial Intelligence (AI) in Online Courses

We would be remiss not to discuss the role and place of AI in online courses and, in particular, translation and interpreting classes. AI is a formidable technology to increase accessibility. Screen readers for visually impaired students, with several tool suggestions offered by the American Foundation for the Blind, and other software such as Read&Write, which offers literacy support including text to speech technology, have revolutionized accessibility in education. Speech recognition (or dictation) tools, which are now embedded in common software such as Microsoft programs, help students for whom writing represents a barrier to learning. Of course, making courses accessible to people with learning or physical limitations goes beyond the use of AI. Most institutions in the United States offer guidance in terms of course design for enhancing accessibility. Guidance in that regard is also provided by instructional designers or content accessibility specialists (Lynch 2020) and can be found online.

AI has also vastly transformed the translation and interpreting industry, as large language service providers have very early on identified AI, especially machine translation (MT) as a way to drastically reduce their costs. Vast numbers of translation projects are now pre-translated with an MT program and many translators have turned into "editors" or "post-editors," which are unfortunate misnomers but go beyond the scope of this chapter. Professional MT tools are also used by some translators as a productivity tool for certain types of texts. It is helpful to consider the place of MT in the translation curriculum as a series of questions. When and how should instructors introduce MT to students? At one specific point in the curriculum? In an iterative manner, considered under different angles, introduced by different instructors? Should it be only introduced in a translation technology course? Should MT be part of an ethics course? Should MT be integrated in all translation courses, as a specific module including ethical questions and practical applications? Recent research shows that the cognitive effort needed to edit an MT-translated text can, for certain types of texts, be higher than the effort needed to translate from scratch. Should instructors cover cognitive aspects as well? And since the standard per word rate is also impacted by the advent of MT, should MT be part of a career development course? These questions, among many others, need to be carefully examined in the design or redesign of any translation curriculum.

The impact of AI in the T&I industry is not limited to MT: Speech recognition software, such as Dragon Naturally Speaking (which dates back to the late '90s), currently owned by Nuance, a Microsoft company, or the embedded speech recognition tool in Microsoft itself, is increasingly favored by translators who, for various reasons including the prevention of repetitive stress injury, wish to type less and dictate their translations instead. It can also be advantageously implemented in a sight translation activity, and more specifically used by students to check their elocution, for instance. New applications of AI in the interpretation industry are currently being experimented with as we write these lines. When discussing what he calls the "Upcoming Technological Turn" in interpreting, Fantiuoli mentions computer assisted interpreting (CAI), remote interpreting (RI), and machine interpreting (MI). CAI includes tools to create glossaries and integrating terminology resources, automatic terminology extraction, key topics identification, summarization, and automatic speech recognition. RI "refers to forms of interpreter-mediated communication delivered by means of information and communication technology" (2019, 4). MI involves automatic speech translation, automatic interpreting, and speech-to-speech interpreting, which make use of the following technologies: automatic speech recognition (ASR), machine translation (MT), and speech-to-text synthesis (STT) to generate an audible version in the target language. Fantinuoli reminds us that the latter is still not able to "work—as yet—with cotext and context or to translate all the information that is not explicitly coded verbally, such as speaker's attitude, world references, etc." (2019, 6). These applications will need to be evaluated and, should they be durably implemented as interpreting tools, introduced to students. Instructors will need to formulate questions similar to the ones regarding MT (see previous discussion) so that students are fully equipped to evaluate these tools under every possible facet.

Finally, because this book is about online education, the authors recognize that by the time this manuscript goes to print, some of the tools and platforms mentioned herein might have changed, products and companies been bought out or acquired a different brand name, or even disappeared from the virtual space altogether. The ever-changing nature of distance learning creates a situation in which educators are currently being bombarded with new remote learning tools, devices, platforms, research, conferences, etc., which should be seen as good news. However, the authors would like to point out that sometimes this feels exhausting and every so often, we as instructors feel we will never be able to catch up. However, we trust that the ideas, concepts, and insights presented herein can be replicated in new environments and even improved as new technologies become available.

References

Afolabi, Segun, and Oludamilola I. Oyetoyan. "Charting a New Course for Translator and Interpreter Training in Africa: Lessons from the COVID-19 Experience in Selected Countries." *The Journal of Specialized Translation*, no. 36b, July 2021, pp. 327–50.

Alim, H. Samy, and Django Paris. "What Is Culturally Sustaining Pedagogy and Why Does It Matter?" *Culturally Sustaining Pedagogies: Teaching and Learning for Justice in a Changing World*. Teachers College Press, 2017.

Azizinezhad, Masoud, and Masoud Hashemi. "The Use of Blogs in Teaching and Learning Translation." *Procedia – Social and Behavioral Sciences*, vol. 28, 2011, pp. 867–71.

Barros Filho, Eduardo A. "A TV Como Escola: O Uso Educativo Da Televisão Pré Ditadura Militar." *Patrimônio e Memória—UNESP*, 2018, http://pem.assis.unesp.br/index.php/pem/article/view/687.

Bilić, Viktorija. "The Online Computer-Assisted Translation Classroom." *The International Journal for Translation & Interpreting Research*, vol. 12, no. 1, 2020, pp. 127–41.

Bond, Esther. "Linguistic Diversity in the US Hits Record High." *Slator*, 2018, https://slator.com/demand-drivers/linguistic-diversity-in-the-us-hits-record-high/.

Chen, Nian-Shing, and Leong Ko. "Online Interpreting Test in Synchronous Cyber Classrooms." *International Workshop on Technology for Education (T4E)*, 2009, pp. 24–31.

Darby, Flower. *Small Teaching Online: Applying Learning Science in Online Classes*. Wiley, 2019.

Fantinuoli, Claudio. *Interpreting and Technology*. Language Science Press, 2019.

Gannon, Kevin. "Teaching Online Will Make You a Better Teacher in Any Setting." *The Chronicle of Higher Education*, Sept. 2019, www.chronicle.com/article/Teaching-Online-Will-Make-You/247031.

Gorozhanov, Alexey I., Elena F. Kosichenko, and Innara A. Guseynova. "Teaching Written Translation Online: Theoretical Model, Software Development, Interim Results." *SHS Web of Conferences*, EDP Sciences, 2018, https://www.shs-conferences.org/articles/shsconf/pdf/2018/11/shsconf_cildiah2018_01062.pdf.

Hlavac, Jim. "Interpreter Credentialing, Testing and Training in Australia: Past, Contemporary and Future Directions." *FITISPos Training and Research in Public Service Translation and Interpreting*, vol. 3, 2016.

"Inclusive and Equitable Teaching—ACUE Curriculum Crosswalk." *Association of Colleges and Universities Educators*, 2020, https://acue.org/wp-content/uploads/2020/10/ACUE-Inclusive-Equitable-Teaching-Crosswalk_singlepage_102820.pdf.

Ladson-Billings, Gloria. "Toward a Theory of Culturally Relevant Pedagogy." *American Educational Research Journal*, vol. 32, no. 3, 1995, pp. 465–91.

Lynch, Laura. "Have You Created an Accessible Online Course?" 4 Apr. 2020, www.learndash.com/have-you-created-an-accessible-online-course/.

"Much-Needed Interpreters on the Horizon." *Karen Organization of Minnesota*, 10 Sept. 2020, www.mnkaren.org/news/much-needed-interpreters-on-the-horizon/.

"Nearly Half of World's Population Excluded from 'Benefits of Digitalization', Speaker Stresses as Second Committee Debates Information Technology for Development." *United Nations*, 18 Oct. 2019, www.un.org/press/en/2019/gaef3523.doc.htm.

Perramon, María, and Xus Ugarte. "Teaching Interpreting Online for the Translation and Interpreting Degree at the University of Vic." *Translation and Translanguaging in Multilingual Contexts*, vol. 6, no. 2, John Benjamins Publishing Company, 2020, pp. 172–82.

"Purdue Repository for Online Teaching and Learning." 2020, www.purdue.edu/innovativelearning/supporting-instruction/portal/files/4_Community_of_Inquiry_Framework.pdf.

Reefer, Kayla. "Anyone Speak K'iche' or Mam? Immigration Courts Overwhelmed by Indigenous Languages." *The New York Times*, 19 Mar. 2019, www.nytimes.com/2019/03/19/us/translators-border-wall-immigration.html.

Sachtleben, Annette. "Pedagogy for the Multilingual Classroom: Interpreting Education." *The International Journal for Translation & Interpreting Research*, vol. 7, no. 2, 2015, pp. 51–9.

Seaman, Julia E., I. Elaine Allen, and Jeff Seaman. "Grade Increase: Tracking Distance Education in the United States." *BABSON Survey Research Group*, https://bayviewanalytics.com/reports/gradeincrease.pdf.

Universal Design for Learning: A Concise Introduction. Colorado State University, http://accessproject.colostate.edu/udl/modules/udl_introduction/udl_concise_intro.pdf.

Weiss, Mike. "Why Students Don't Complete Your Online Course (and 5 Ways to Fix It)." 25 Mar. 2019, www.clientengagementacademy.com/blog/students-dont-complete-online-course/.

2 Process-Oriented and Skill-Building Pedagogy

This chapter starts from the assumption that translation and interpreting are skills that exist alongside different levels of bilingualism or multilingualism, and as such develop over time as a result of practice.

2.1 Translation

Birgitta Englund differentiates two types of translation ability: 1) basic; that of an individual who is able to perform translation as a consequence of simply knowing more than one language, and 2) professional; that of an individual's ability to perform translation competently—which includes several sub-competences, as in knowledge of source languages (SL) and target languages (TL) and cultures, pragmatic and stylistic knowledge of the two languages, subject matter knowledge or advanced translation research skills (dictionaries, term banks, the Internet, parallel texts, etc.), competence in writing, and computer-related skills (word processors, computer-assisted translation [CAT] tools, automatic translation software, etc.) (2005, 30–3). Even though Englund makes reference to translators having to make decisions when translating, she does not mention translation ethics as one of the sub-competences of professional translators, which the authors of this book strongly believe should be added to the list. More on the importance of incorporating ethics in educational translation and interpreting initiatives, and in particular, online learning, is discussed in Chapter 6.

When discussing the process of translation in his textbook *Becoming a Translator: An Introduction to the Theory and Practice of Translation*, Douglas Robinson alludes to practice as a condition for reaching the so-called "subliminal stage" in which translators work faster and more productively by breaking down the different stages they go through to acquire experience and develop translation skills. Borrowing from Charles Sanders Peirce's abduction, induction, and deduction triad, Robinson (2020) states,

> novice translators begin by approaching a text with an instructive sense that they know how to do this . . . with their first actual experience of

DOI: 10.4324/9781003149316-3

a text they realize that they don't know how to proceed, but take an abductive guess anyway; and soon are translating away, learning inductively as they go, by trial and error, making mistakes and learning from those mistakes; they gradually deduce patterns and regularities that help them to translate faster and more effectively; and eventually these patterns and regularities become habit or second nature, are incorporated into a subliminal activity of which they are occasionally aware.

(59)

Robinson's quote also highlights the importance of instructors creating safe spaces for students to make mistakes and offering opportunities for fixing and reflecting on them. In one of the online translation courses taught by one of the authors, students are first asked to work on a first draft of a translation and submit it with a reflection on the process they used to search for the target translation of the source term or phrase that took them the longest to resolve. Students receive feedback on their reflection and translated text and are then asked to work on a "final" version. At the end of the course, while building their final portfolio, students are invited to reflect on all the feedback they received in all their assignments during the semester and look for patterns (i.e., grammatical issues, inappropriate target translation solutions, etc.) and evidence that they have incorporated feedback and improved their performance. Robinson's use of Pierce's model also brings to the fore something that is not much discussed in translation classrooms, the idea that intuition is a very productive force. Most traditional translation courses will teach students to never guess or intuit the target translation of a particular source term or phrase; that they should always start with research. This unfortunately does two things: It does not recognize students' realities—i.e., most will start with guessing—and prevents instructors and students from talking about the constructive force of intuition; of approaching a translation challenge with one's pre-existing knowledge to then moving to the final stage of confirmation.

2.2 Interpreting

As far as interpreting is concerned, Moser-Mercer has written extensively about the task as a performance skill. In "Skill Acquisition in Interpreting: A Human Performance Perspective," when discussing the cognitive and meta-cognitive processes necessary in interpreter education, Moser-Mercer reminds us that, "skill acquisition relies heavily on practice and experience, which produce cognitive changes that facilitate the circumvention of cognitive constraints inherent in highly complex tasks such as simultaneous interpreting" (2008, 7). As educators know, interpreting students must develop a number of processes and sub-tasks to be able to perform at high levels, making use of different strategies including anticipation, summarizing, chunking, and paraphrasing.

To explain how novice interpreters transition to experts, Manuela Motta states, "the acquisition of expert performance . . . requires a systematic and deliberate approach" to practice (2011, 32). Teachers or coaches should include scaffolding considerations for various types of exercises when designing online training and educational activities. Motta reminds instructors that students must have access to well-defined tasks and that they need opportunities to improve performance by working on the same or similar exercises repeatedly. Moreover, students should also remember that such practice should be limited to a specific amount of time per day to avoid exhaustion, since it requires maximum concentration. Motta also discusses the importance of feedback in students' journeys in developing interpreting and meta-cognitive skills, "not only does deliberate practice require the student's maximum concentration and cooperation, but students should also develop meta-cognitive and self-regulatory skills so that they can self-evaluate themselves when tutors or teachers are no longer available to provide them with feedback" (33). Meta-cognition is one of the cornerstones of deliberate practice, allowing students to become aware of their own knowledge, controlling and improving their interpreting skills.

Instructors should heed Motta's advice when designing online translation and interpreting courses and should incorporate the three components she suggests as necessary to the development of skills and meta-cognition: "modeling, scaffolding, and reflection,"

> Modelling consists in providing opportunities for students to observe expert practice; scaffolding consists in providing support for specific aspects of the task which students find particularly difficult, and reflection provides leaners with a means of externalizing their meta-cognitive processes and thus evaluating them.
>
> (34)

2.3 Self-Regulated Students

Such a concept also agrees with educational initiatives framed by socio-constructivism, which places students in the center of the process and occurs in collaboration with instructors and their peers through feedback, while introducing them to principles of autonomous learning in order to allow them to analyze their own performance as they progress in their educational and professional journeys. Self-regulation through reflective practice (journals, short reflections, rubrics, etc.) sets students up to develop the lifelong learning skills they will need as they transition to professional lives.

In the spirit of placing students in the center of the learning process, the authors conducted an informal survey among students taking different online translation and interpreting courses at the University of Massachusetts Amherst in June 2021, to grasp their understanding of the reflective practice methodology (Jay-Rayon Ibrahim Aibo and Mazzei 2021). Three questions about their experiences with homework-related reflections were sent out to 61 students taking online summer classes at the institution via an online survey platform called SurveyMonkey, and slightly over 50% of them responded (30). The vast majority of respondents (27) had positive things to say about their metalinguistic engagement with their translation and interpreting exercises:

- "great way to practice critical thinking"
- "helped me be aware of my mistakes and think of strategies to improve"
- "makes me be more mindful and attentive towards the process of translating"
- "confirms aspects of my process that I wanted to continue implementing in the future and redirected me from aspects that didn't serve me well"
- "helped me to see how important it is to follow specific steps in order to produce a faithful interpretation/translation"
- "helps me identify some final adjustments to improve my work"
- "I get to share with my instructor my thought process"
- "contribute to promoting self-awareness"
- "much easier to pinpoint areas of improvement"
- "prompt a deeper analysis"
- "makes me look back and work on my weaknesses"
- "the thinking process was kind of cathartic"
- "biggest takeaway is to be able to see one's progress"
- "these kinds of epiphanies only occur when one is forced to think things through analytically"
- "building confidence to face the real world"
- "learned how to analyze text and speech by breaking down its components"

As can be inferred from the listed comments, students are incorporating important metalinguistic skills about their performances that will serve them well in their professional lives. Moreover, they are actively involved in their learning process toward becoming self-regulated students, professionals, and citizens. When explaining her view of self-regulated learning, Linda Nilson states, "learning is about one's relationship with oneself and one's ability to exert the effort, self-control, and critical self-assessment necessary to achieve the best possible results—and about overcoming risk aversion, failure, distractions, and sheer laziness in pursuit of *real* achievement" (2015, xxvii). Nilson's book, grounded on self-efficacy and social cognition theories (Zimmerman and Schunk 2001), offers strategies to improve students' self-awareness and emotional self-regulation about their learning process, many of which will be highlighted in the next section.

2.4 Reflective Practice

Another important component of deliberate practice is defining clear tasks, identifying problems and the causes behind them, and coming up with strategies to address them. When calling for a systemic approach to learning and practice in interpreter training, Rachel Herring states that developing skills "tends to be more efficient when the task is broken down into smaller units that can be addressed separately during training" (2015, 20). In quoting K. Anders Ericsson (2000), a researcher in expertise and skill acquisition, Herring reminds us of the important role of motivation, feedback, and repeated practice for interpreting skills development.

The more obvious way to foster meta-cognitive skills in translation and interpreting students is to require them to produce journals, reflections, and self-assessment of their practice. Encouraging students to reflect on their process of tackling translation and interpreting challenges, applying research strategies, identifying and using terminology tools, etc. lends itself very well to multilingual online courses since students will be writing (or submitting their reflections via voice/video) in the pivot language being used in the classes or the language of learning and teaching (LoLT), which, in the case of the authors of this book, is English. Regardless of the language pair, when analyzing students' reflections, instructors develop a deep understanding of their processes and are able to guide them accordingly through appropriate feedback, encouraging students to think critically about their work and incorporate such observation in their journey to becoming professionals in the field and beyond. The following are some illustrations of instruments currently used by the authors that foster such instructor-student and peer-to-peer collaborations.

2.5 Reflections on the Translation Process

Conventional translation training has long been based on the transmission of knowledge from instructors to students, with instructors asking students to translate a text and then going over their errors focusing on "translation problems," to finally presenting the "correct" way to translate, with very little participation from students and limited discussions about what happens during the process of translation (Kiraly 2000). This changed somewhat in the 1990s with research using think-aloud protocols (TAPs) aimed at investigating differences in the performance of professional and novice translators, and to collect information on the cognitive process of translation, which then began to be incorporated sparingly into translator training. With such research available, some educators started to explore ways through which they could encourage their students to reflect on the process of translating mostly after the fact (not during the translational activity), since in a classroom environment, the controlled structure of a TAP could not be widely applied, least so in an online environment.

In online education, students are able to explore different formats with which to submit the analyses of their own performance, including traditional written reflections in word processing files submitted to a specific area inside the LMS. However, instructors and students have at their disposal a wide variety of formats that can be used for such reflective practice. Most LMS platforms, such as Moodle and Blackboard, offer spaces for students to submit journals which can be easily graded and commented on (instructors can even determine if such journaling should be individual or shared with the entire class for collaborative work). Moreover, for online classes where writing is not the main focus, such as many interpreting courses, students can produce their reflections using video, voice, or images. VoiceThread, for example, which will be discussed in more detail in Chapter 3, is a robust tool offering teachers and students opportunities to interact in different ways. For video or audio recording, students can use web-based platforms such as Screencast-O-Matic or even PowerPoint with embedded narration of slides.

However, to be able to reflect and self-assess, students must be introduced to the different steps involved in the process of a task, as mentioned previously. For example, when it comes to written translation, breaking down the activity into clear and distinct operations allows students to narrow their focus while translating and prepare them to reflect on their performance after completing the task. Using the framework proposed by McTighe and Wiggins in *Essential Questions: Opening Doors to Student Understanding*, such steps can be introduced through questions, shifting the role of the instructor from the one who has all the answers to the one facilitating the inquiry (2013, 87). The following section shows an example through which the different stages in the translation process can be divided and introduced to students in an online class through questions.

2.5.1 Translation Process Steps

Source meaning:

- What do I know about the subject matter of this text?
- How do I know what this word/term means in this context? Did I look it up in a monolingual dictionary? Online or offline?
- What else can I learn about this word/term? Did I Google it being used in context?
- Did I attempt to use my intuition and guess what it means? Did I proceeded to look it up in a bilingual dictionary? Did I follow up to confirm that my guess was correct?

Target translation:

- Now that I know what it means in the source language, did I look up its target translation in a bilingual dictionary? Online or offline?

- Did I check to see if the source term already has a standardized target translation available?
- Since I couldn't find the target translation in any bilingual dictionary, did I try to find the potential synonyms for the word/term? Did I use an online thesaurus? Offline?
- Did I look up the target term in a different closely related language using a bilingual dictionary?
- Did I search for the term on the database of an online translator's forum (online)? Proz.com? TranslatorsCafé? WordReference?
- I couldn't find it in their database. Did I post a question to one of those forums? Which one? Did anyone reply? Was I satisfied with the solution? Did I remember to thank the person who proposed the target translation?
- Did I search both the source and target terms on Google? Was the target term being used in the same context? Did I use Google Images? Did I search for the target translation in parallel texts? Which ones?
- Did I ask a subject matter expert for help? Did I ask a friend who speaks both languages? Did I ask a family member? How reliable was the answer? What makes me confident that the expert knew the target translation?

In the spirit of the UDL framework, as discussed in Chapter 1, such information can be introduced to students in the simple format of written questions, such as those listed previously, or presented as a "mind map" with the use of an online platform that can be used to organize and present ideas. Students are then asked to write a short reflection addressing the ways through which they searched for and found the best solution for their translation unit or map out their process using an online mind-mapping platform.[1] If instructors request a written reflection, an exemplar should always be provided to students as a guiding document. This harks back to the concept of modeling discussed earlier as part of introducing students to acceptable levels of engagement with the activity, in which educators provide students with a template that makes the expectations for the task clear. The following section shows an example.

2.5.2 Translation Process Reflection

"Term or Phrase: XXXXX

1. To begin with, I needed to make sure I understood the term "xxxxx." In my head, it meant xxxxx, but I wanted confirmation of that, so I looked up "xxxxx" in a monolingual dictionary (provide URL or print source). The difficulty with this word is that it is generally a noun, but in our context, it's a verb. I found an unclear definition, so I then went to thesaurus.com and found some synonyms such as the verbs *xxxxx*, *xxxxx*, *xxxxx*, and *xxxxx*.

Process-Oriented & Skill-Building Pedagogy 37

2   Next, I went to a bilingual dictionary in my language pair, xxxxx (provide URL or print source). There is only one translation listed for "xxxxx" as a verb (*xxxxxx*). I'm concerned this may be too literal, plus it appears that the context for this verb is different than the context of the source language term. It could be correct, but more research is needed. Next, I went to Proz.com. I tried a couple of different combinations in my search. "xxxx xxxxx" did not bring up any helpful results but "xxxx xxxxx" brought up two helpful results in the context. I found various possible translations: *xxxxx, xxxxx, xxxxx, xxxxx, xxxxx*.

3   To confirm the right word, I went to the monolingual Spanish dictionary, RAE (www.rae.es/). Although I really like the translation *xxxx xxxxx* since it's very specific, I think I would be changing the register by using it. They could have written "xxxx xxxxx" in the article if they had wanted. On RAE, I looked up *xxxxx, xxxxx*, and *xxxxx*. I really think that *xxxxx*'s definition is what we are referring to here. To confirm further, I went to Google España (www.google.es/) and looked up combinations of those three verbs with the word *xxxxx* in collocating dictionaries, such as www.corpusdelespanol.org/. Finally, I find an article from the *Academia Mexicana de Lengua* that explains how *xxxxx* and *xxxxx* are used in regard to economics, which helps me to rule out those two verbs as options."

As mentioned previously, free online web-based platforms can also be used to illustrate the translation process in synchronous or asynchronous classes. If the concept is being introduced in a live online meeting, instructors can then break students into groups and have them work on one specific translation challenge and then produce a mind map of the process they went through in order to find the best target translation. This can also be done as an asynchronous activity with students submitting the link to where their map is hosted. Figure 2.1 is an image of a reflection example created by one of the authors of this book using the MindMup platform (www.mindmup.com/).

After having explored the different steps in the process of translation, students should be ready to engage in deeper reflections about their work. In the example that follows, they are asked to translate a short text, selected by the instructor, from English into their Language Other Than English (LOTE) in a specific field of knowledge, for instance, health care. After completing their work, they are invited to write a short reflection in English on their process guided by a rubric. Students are told this will be their first draft of the translation and that after receiving feedback, they must go back to their translations and work on the final version while incorporating the individual feedback provided by the instructor. The authors of this book address rubrics in more details in Chapter 5, but suffice to say that such tools allow students to develop critical thinking skills regarding their

38 Process-Oriented & Skill-Building Pedagogy

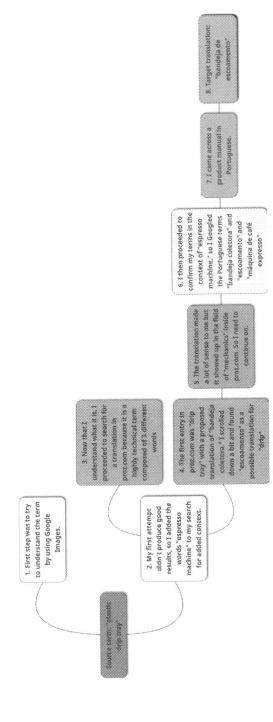

Figure 2.1 Mind Map of Translation Process to Find Portuguese Target Translation of English Term "Plastic Drip Tray"
Source: Mazzei (2021)

progress and performance and provide a roadmap for them to reflect on their practice.

"Health Care Translation
You are encouraged to translate this short text (URL added); submit the first draft to the appropriate box on (name of LMS) (the file should be saved and named as "**healthcare_yourname_draft**"). You will receive feedback on your process and then you will have one more week to work on the final draft, which must be submitted to the appropriate box on (name of LMS) by the posted deadline (file should be saved and named as "**healthcare_yourname_final**"). Your first draft should be accompanied by a short reflection on the process and steps you took to resolve *one* specific translation challenge or unit (a word, a term, or a phrase). For an example of the reflection, see the document "Translation_Reflection_Model" in your online shell. Also, as you write your reflection, use the rubric posted online and address some of the questions raised by your instructor."

This reflective exercise encourages students to analyze the process and allows the instructors to provide feedback on it, pointing them in the right direction in terms of developing lifelong learning skills and consolidating translation concepts. More importantly, in addition to being individual, the feedback can also be shared with the entire class. The added advantage of multilingual classes is that, when reading their classmates' reflections, students are exposed to different ways of addressing similar translation challenges from different linguistic and cultural perspectives. For example, a student working in the English-Spanish pair might use a different strategy when encountering a translation challenge than a student working in the English-Hmong pair and will benefit very much from learning how Hmong speakers make much more use of explicitation or paraphrasing when tackling scientific and health care terms. The following is an example where the instructor extracted individual feedback given on the reflections of different students with different language combinations, anonymized them, pasted them all together into a portable document format (PDF) document, and shared it with the entire class.

"General Feedback on Students' Translations for the Entire Class:
- "For Hmong there's a need to unpack/explain English terms in order to come up with the best translation solutions. The federal agency CDC (Centers for Disease Control and Prevention), for example, could be paraphrased as the Government Department that Controls/Manages/Supervises Diseases . . . right?"
- "Please, avoid using Google Translate. As you indicate in your research of an Arabic equivalent for 'frail,' you should have started your process by first looking the term up in an English dictionary to fully understand it in this context, which should be 'having delicate health;' 'not robust;' 'weak.' After understanding the source meaning, you can then

- proceed to looking up equivalents in Arabic. Some good online sources are *Almaany* and *Sensagent*. Another good source for Arabic medical terms is the *Mufasser*."
- "Please focus your research on ONE term only. If you selected 'discharge' as a term to reflect on, don't talk about other terms such as 'flu-like,' which by the way is NOT a technical term."
- "Don't worry if the target translation is longer. Languages have different structures/syntax and you should follow them. Usually, when translating from English to a Romance language (such as Spanish, Portuguese, Italian, French, etc.), there's an increase in the number of words used in the target language."
- "I'm glad you went back to your translation after a day or two. This is a very good strategy if you have the time."
- "This is what I found quickly when I researched 'stuffy head' online. It is a headache, maybe due to stuffy nose. Popular: My head is stuffy—Scientific: Acute sinusitis—What causes this stuffiness? A sinus infection could be the cause of head stuffiness."
- "Very good research. I'm glad you used a parallel text from a reputable source to find the translation for the term you decided to write about: CDC (Center for Disease Control)."
- "I'm glad you read parallel texts in the target language before you started your translation. Good job."
- "Be careful with *Linguee* . . . it shows you 'translated' texts and not parallel texts, which are originally written in the target language."
- "Good reflection. However, when you're selecting the best translation for your term you have to take into consideration the register. 'Runny nose' is a popular term in English. So, you need to find a popular term in the target language and keep the register. You ended up selecting a scientific term, and therefore, changed the register.'"

As can be seen in the example above, the shared feedback document can be reused in the following iterations of the same online class, since many patterns observed in novice translators' learning journeys repeat themselves time and time again—e.g., trying to find a target translation before fully understanding the source term, using unreliable sources to find equivalents, not considering registers, falling into the trap of literal translation, etc. The process-oriented feedback also includes and should include notes on students' successful performance and strategies, producing important takeaways that all students can incorporate into their translation skills, such as the importance of using parallel texts and reliable dictionaries. Instructor feedback that only focuses on errors and mistakes will lead to students feeling discouraged about their learning processes.

Another way to share knowledge and promote collaborative learning is to ask students to reflect on their translation process together on a living document, such as a Google Doc (or any other online collaborative tool, such as

Padlet, etc.). This can be done synchronously during a live meeting. If this is an asynchronous activity, instructors should, of course, establish a deadline for when such contributions must be submitted.

2.6 Reflective Practice in Interpreting

Now let us turn our attention to an example of reflective practice for an interpreting assignment.

Based on clear instructions and context, students are asked to record their interpretation, listen to it, and write a reflection or a self-assessment based on a rubric. The exercise is long consecutive interpreting (CI) with note-taking. In online interpreting classes, instructors should provide clear instructions about the kinds of recording device to be used and the expectations regarding audio quality, file extension, size, naming, etc. For example, for optimal results, students should record themselves in a quiet space, without background noise or interruptions. Freeware software programs, such as Audacity, can be utilized, as well as digital recording devices and even good quality smart phones.

"**Instructions for Long Consecutive Interpretation with Notes:**
Perform consecutive interpreting with note-taking from a short oral passage. **Prepare and Practice:** Before attempting to work on this assignment, review the materials under "Practice Materials" and prepare. Read the materials, come up with symbols and abbreviations as learned throughout the course; practice on audio files of the same topic; ask your classmates to record short audio files that you can use for practice, etc. Under the **VoiceThread** "Long Consecutive Safe Practice Space," students are invited and encouraged to submit audio files about the topic so that their classmates can practice on it! **Assignment:** Play and listen to the audio file provided in the link once, take notes, and record your interpretation of the source speech based on your notes and memory. Submit your audio file, an image (picture) of your notes (you can also use your smart phone), and your short reflection based on the rubric. You should submit at least three different files total. Reflections can be written or oral (audio file)."

Again, the concept of rubrics will be described in Chapter 6, but the following example is a written reflection template (an example of student prior work) that can be shared with students so that they have a clear idea of the expectation from the instructor regarding the acceptable level of reflective practice for this specific exercise:

"**Meaning Distortions**
I believe meaning was mostly conveyed. I interpreted "bottom line" as xxxx (the last point), which is not the ideal target translation. While listening to my recording I found a couple grammar mistakes.
Omissions/Additions
I felt that I interpreted the most important ideas of the text but I did not go sentence by sentence. When listening to my CI, I could not think of how to

say certain words in my target language, for example "mucus flow freely." So I paraphrased a bit and came up with xxxxxx xxxx xxxx xxxxxx (which means "mucus will break down and drain easily"). On the other hand, for some reason, while rendering "which increase mucus production," I added, "this can be annoying" which was not on the tape. Where did that come from? I should be more careful not to add unnecessary information (or my own personal views) in my interpretation.

Delivery

I did have some hesitations, some *uhhhs*, particularly during the introduction and on difficult terms because I couldn't read my notes clearly sometimes. A few times, I did go back and corrected myself or provided a better term.

Patterns/Problems

1. Poor note-taking skills; concentration & memory; 2. Target language grammar; 3. Hesitancy.

Improvement Plans

I should practice more my note taking to improve my CI to free up some of my cognitive efforts. I also need to feel more relaxed and confident while interpreting because otherwise, I will lose my focus and my memory. When I listened to my recording, I noticed my breathing was loud. I should try to sit up straight to improve my breathing."

As can be seen in these examples, the task (CI) has been broken down into smaller parts—meaning errors, omissions/additions, delivery, and patterns/problems—making it easier for students to focus on different aspects of their performance as they listen to their recording. Moreover, one part invites students to design plans for improvement based on issues they have identified themselves, which is part of the framework to foster lifelong learning and continuing education toward professional expertise. In addition, their reflection can be individual, as in submitted to and visible only by instructors, or shared with the rest of the class with students' permission or by removing identifiable information. Students can also submit their reflections in oral form or video through the use of VoiceThread, for example, or other web-based freeware or as part of the LMS instructors are working with.

2.7 Multilingual T&I Classes

Obviously, the examples provided can be applied to online language-specific translation and interpreting classes. However, as pointed out in "Translation and Interpreting Pedagogy" by Colina and Angelelli, educational programs in the field are increasingly focusing on the needs of "more diverse student populations, characterized by varying levels of language proficiency and translation and interpreting competence" (2016, 114). Diversity in terms of students' languages and cultures is closely tied to immigration trends around the world, especially in wealthier nations, and translation and interpreting courses are having to respond to the increased need for training students who speak languages of lesser diffusion (LLD). Different countries around the world currently have laws or mandates with language access provisions, making it mandatory (or at least strongly recommended) for institutional settings to provide translation and interpreting services to immigrants so that they, in turn, are able to access the public services they are entitled to and fully participate in society. The authors of this book contend that designing multilingual classes can and should meet such needs.

Moreover, the concept of community translation, as proposed by Taibi and Ozolins, seems to resonate very well with multilingual translation and interpreting courses and the need to rethink pedagogies. "[G]eneralist translation programmes are a good starting point for community translators, but training specifically addressing community contexts would be more efficient and relevant" (2016, 24). Taibi and Ozolins also point out that the activity occurs in multilingual and multicultural communities,

> where disempowered groups such as migrants, refugees or local ethnic minorities do not have access to texts written in the mainstream language(s). In such contexts it is often the case that the difference between the mainstream audience and the users of community translations is not only linguistic, but also socio-economic, cultural and educational.
>
> (13)

Maria Tymoczko (2014), in *Enlarging Translation, Empowering Translators*, challenges Western notions of translation and meaning conversion and invites scholars and educators to explore and research non-Western translation practices to expand the definition of the practice. Encouraging students who speak non-Western languages in a multilingual class to share their strategies to tackle meaning conversion between two or more languages seems to meet the challenge proposed by Tymoczko, at least when it comes to inviting different ways of conceptualizing meaning and what works for different cultures and languages. In turn, students working with languages of wider diffusion can benefit from and perhaps challenge their own prescriptive translation norms.

Calling for an interactive approach that encourages student participation and dialogue, Maria González Davies states that "in consonance with postcolonial times, concepts such as catering for diversity, multicultural and multilinguistic teaching, respect for the learner and for learning and teaching styles have become commonplace" (2004, 13). Based on socioconstructivist principles, Davies proposes the engagement of students in the learning process and offers different types of activities that can be used with different language combinations. Even though Davies states that readers of her book can adapt her ideas to any language combination, she does not mention multilingual classes—in which students come from different cultural and linguistic backgrounds and engage with each other through a common language of learning and teaching. However, her multiple voices framework is very useful to language-neutral translation and interpreting education, especially when instructors are invited to forego the idea that their classrooms are composed of a homogenous group of students. In multilingual classes, heterogeneity is the norm, not only in terms of language combinations but also in terms of cultural norms, ways of approaching education, making sense of the world, and translation and interpreting in their specific contexts. Davies also grounds her proposed activities and projects on the idea that translation is a skill students will develop as they focus on their learning journeys, which should be based on helping students "move from the most rudimentary level of the word to the more complicated issues of syntax and, finally, to those of cultural difference" (17).

As mentioned earlier, many students working in multilingual courses speak minority languages or LLDs and face several challenges that are somewhat different from other languages of wider diffusion. Some of those languages and cultures are based on oral traditions and have been written down by European missionaries or linguists. Some of them are based on spiritual beliefs that often clash with those of their new host countries. Some of their classmates are speakers of "powerful languages," as defined by the World Economic Forum in 2016, such as Spanish, French, German, etc. and, as such, have access to a wealth of resources they can use in their translation and interpreting exercises (dictionaries, parallel texts, practice materials, etc.) (Chan 2016). Some students' ethnicities are tied to colonial and postcolonial histories of their classmates' ancestors. Moreover, most translation and interpreting theories and pedagogies have originated in the West; precepts, norms, techniques, strategies, and resources have been geared to (and produced by) languages that are more widely spread because of their current or past powerful economic positions in the world, and therefore are not always applicable to language combinations in which one of them is an LLD. For example, according to Anne Fadiman (1998), the title of her book *The Spirit Catches You and You Fall Down* is actually the Hmong translation of the medical term "epilepsy." How can Western translation strategies explain and aid students that must make use of different ways to carry meaning over to the target language that account for the cultural and spiritual beliefs of their own cultures? How can meaning be reconstructed back to the source language, as in the case of dialogue interpreting, if such circuitous translation strategies are used and have not yet been standardized?

2.8 T&I Teaching Materials for Multilingual Classes

Moreover, the little pedagogy available for translator and interpreter training often needs to be adapted to multilingual settings where community translation and interpreting takes center stage, and where many minority languages and LLDs are more commonly used. On the one hand, instructors work hard to adapt materials, strategies, and concepts designed for areas such as conference interpreting to community and dialogue settings. On the other hand, this is also a great opportunity to invite students to participate in the co-construction of course content, assignments, syllabi, rubrics, classroom etiquette, etc. Instructors can also encourage LLD students to build and share resources, design role-plays, produce audio recordings that can be used for interpreting practice, etc. Moreover, in situations when there is only one LLD student in the group, an advantage of online translation and interpreting courses is that it is easier to connect them to other institutions within the same country or abroad, and even to members of multilingual community organizations.

The authors of this book firmly believe that the rich multilingual and multicultural environment of the language-neutral classroom benefits students working both in languages of lesser and wider diffusion as they learn from each other different strategies that can be applied to translation and interpreting challenges and different perspectives of how to carry meaning over to different cultures. Another important rationale for combining different populations of students is due to cost and enrollment issues, since many high-quality programs or certificates in higher education cannot afford to run language-specific classes with small groups of students for combinations that are in dire need of training to meet the demands of community translation and interpreting.

Note

1 https://elearningindustry.com/the-5-best-free-mind-mapping-tools-for-teachers.

References

Chan, Kai. "These Are the Most Powerful Languages in the World." *World Economic Forum*, 2 Dec. 2016, https://www.weforum.org/agenda/2016/12/these-are-the-most-powerful-languages-in-the-world/.
Colina, Sonia, and Claudia Angelelli. "Translation and Interpreting Pedagogy." *Researching Translation and Interpreting*, edited by Claudia Angelelli and Brian James Baer, Taylor & Francis, 2016.
Davies, Maria Gonzalez. *Multiple Voices in the Translation Classroom*. John Benjamins, 2004.
Dimitrova Englund, Birgitta. *Expertise and Explicitation in the Translation Process*. John Benjamins Publishing Company, 2005.
Ericsson, K. Anders. "Expertise in Interpreting: An Expert-Performance Perspective." *Interpreting*, vol. 5, no. 2, 2000.
Fadiman, Anne. *The Spirit Catches You and You Fall Down: A Hmong Child, Her Doctors, and the Collision of Two Cultures*. Farrar, Straus and Giroux, 1998.
Herring, Rachel. "A Deliberate Practice Approach to Skill Development." *The ATA Chronicle*, June 2015, www.ata-chronicle.online/wp-content/uploads/4406_19_herring.pdf.
Jay-Rayon, Laurence Ibrahim Aibo, and Cristiano Mazzei. *Role of Reflections in Your Progress*. Survey, SurveyMonkey, 8 June 2021.

Kiraly, Don. *A Social Constructivist Approach to Translator Education: Empowerment from Theory to Practice*. St. Jerome, 2000.

Mazzei, Cristiano. Mind Map of Translation Process to Find Portuguese Target Translation of English Term "Plastic Drip Tray." 2021, https://www.mindmup.com/.

McTighe, Jay, and Grant P. Wiggins. *Essential Questions: Opening Doors to Student Understanding*. ASCD, 2013.

Moser-Mercer, Barbara. "Skill Acquisition in Interpreting: A Human Performance Perspective." *The Interpreter and Translator Trainer*, vol. 2, no. 1, 2008, pp. 1–28.

Motta, M. "Facilitating the Novice to Expert Transition in Interpreter Training: A 'Deliberate Practice' Framework Proposal." *Studia UBB Philologia*, vol. 56, no. 1, 2011, pp. 27–42.

Nilson, L.B. *Creating Self-Regulated Learners: Strategies to Strengthen Students' Self-Awareness and Learning Skills*. Stylus Publishing, 2015.

Robinson, Douglas. *Becoming a Translator: An Introduction to the Theory and Practice of Translation*. Fourth, Routledge, 2020.

Taibi, Mustapha, and Uldis Ozolins. *Community Translation*. Bloomsbury, 2016.

Tymoczko, Maria. *Enlarging Translation. Empowering Translators*. Routledge, 2014.

Zimmerman, B.J., and D.H. Schunk. *Self-Regulated Learning and Academic Achievement: Theoretical Perspectives*. Lawrence Erlbaum Associates, 2001.

3 Online Course Development

This chapter focuses on the development phase of online courses. Since course design is dependent on the instructor's approach to teaching, we would like to remind our readers of our underlying approach to educating translators and interpreters. In his paper, "The self-directed learner: intentionality in translator training and education," Kelly Washbourne (2013) documents ways to foster intentional learning and learner autonomy, the two principles that lay the foundation of our own approach and are the focus of this chapter.

In teaching T&I students to learn how to learn, which is part of the new approaches to teaching that emerged in the 21st century (Washbourne 2013, 373), instructors assume a very different role from the one espousing the conventional paradigm of an expert (the instructor) passing down information to non-experts (students). From the students' point of view, self-directed learning points to "movements away from isolated learning and into communities of practice" (Washbourne 2013, 374), and encompasses the goal of achieving autonomy through meaningful interactions with peers and other members of their professional community, away from teacher dependency. Self-directed learning involves relations to others; it calls upon self-management and accountability toward others, envisions instructor and students as "co-creators of the learning environment and motivation" (Washbourne 2013, 374), and embraces the prospect of envisioning learners as future peers of the instructor.

This vision of teaching and learning needs to be communicated very clearly and very early on to learners, since online instruction by definition allows enrollment of students from all over the world, including individuals whose learning environment may not have prepared them to embrace this model. Group participation, critical thinking, self-reflection, and self-evaluation, to name but a few aspects that are in line with this instructional model, might represent dimensions not encouraged in specific regions of the world where students are rather expected to learn content exclusively from their instructor.

In this new model of intentional learning, instructors are envisioned as providing guidance toward agency and autonomy and are training learners

DOI: 10.4324/9781003149316-4

"to take ownership of learning as much as [they are] creating the conditions conducive to translator competence" (Washbourne 2013, 377). A strong focus on process as opposed to end product is therefore paramount to achieve student autonomy and students' ownership toward their continuing education process. The online learning environment represents a formidable opportunity both to enhance the co-construction of learning and to achieve professional verisimilitude.

3.1 Practices and Tools

3.1.1 Learning Stations or Safe Practice Spaces

Learning stations are "ideal for differentiated learning and self-pacing, remediation, group or independent work, tutoring, task breakdown, learning cells, jigsaw collaboration, and more" (Washbourne 2013, 378). Safe practice spaces serve similar purposes and are in line with the US teaching philosophy and concept of "safe spaces" in academia, which can point to either *academic* safe spaces where students are encouraged to take risks in classroom settings or to *organizations* or *physical* spaces on campuses that provide emotional security for marginalized groups (Yee, n.d.). Online safe practice spaces are meant to encourage students to take risks and make mistakes in order to learn from them and overcome their own blocks or fears. They are designed as group spaces in which every student can, for instance, practice a particular interpreting skill, or work on a specific aspect of the translation process, receive feedback and encouragement from their peers, and observe and comment on their peers' own practices. At the same time, these spaces can be used by students to take risks and venture into more complex or more challenging aspects of their practice. As pointed out by Campbell (1991, 339) and Washbourne (2013, 380), challenge-seeking and risk-taking behaviors are desired attitudes in a translator.

3.1.2 Self-Reflections

This instrument may take the form of a guided reflection based on a rubric for a specific task or assignment, or of an individual practice journal. Self-reflections can be designed as individual submissions or shared-access submissions for the benefit of the entire classroom. Shared-access submissions can be designed in different ways. Allowing students to access their peers' submissions once they have submitted their own assignment is but one of various possible reflection assignment designs. Self-reflections are thoroughly discussed in Chapter 2.

3.1.3 Self-Evaluations

In the same vein as self-reflections previously provided, students perform a self-diagnosis using categories from a rubric relating to both process and end product. Self-evaluations are part of the various instruments that help students map their own progress and align their development to learning goals. This is demonstrated and illustrated in Chapter 5.

3.1.4 Selection of Readings

As pointed out by Jafar (2016), engaging students with the selection of readings is a highly effective tool for boosting their commitment and motivation. One way of achieving it in an online setting, where most (if not all) of the course content is usually structured before the start of the course itself, is to ask students to vote week after week on readings that align best with the course learning goals, and those that help them best progress through their personal learning journey, for instance, in order to reorganize readings from one semester to another.

3.2 Writing a Syllabus

One of the big decisions that instructors in online programs face is whether to write the syllabus first, then develop the course content in the LMS itself, or to develop both at the same time. One of the downsides of the second option is that any change made upon reviewing the syllabus will need to be reflected in the course structure in the LMS. A middle-way approach is to create learning modules and their internal architecture (i.e., readings, lectures, discussions, assignments, etc.) within the LMS as the syllabus is being written, without developing the module content.

In face-to-face classes, where, according to Flower Darby in *Small Teaching Online*, "students are well familiarized to the norms of classroom education" (2019, xviii), instructors often spend a considerable amount of time going over course content, goals, assignments, readings, etc. Conversely, syllabi designed for an online environment, where "instructors and other students are not physically present to help guide or shape an online student's behavior," (Darby 2019, xviii), need to be as detailed as possible, especially for fully asynchronous courses where regular virtual meetings between students and instructors are not incorporated into the instruction. Instructors might want to explore the possibility of student co-constructed syllabi. Course evaluations or short surveys at the end of the semester can be used to prompt students to contribute ideas regarding assessments, readings, tasks performed, and even deadlines, and their feedback can help modify future course iterations. For further reference, Blinne outlines a framework for incorporating students' input into the design of course content, more specifically focused on the syllabus (2013).

While we touch upon incorporating virtual meetings to asynchronous courses in the section discussing student engagement, most asynchronous courses are designed to enhance flexibility from the learner's perspective and take into account their busy professional and family schedule, which is one of the main reasons why they chose the asynchronous format in the first place, along with being far from institutions where such courses are offered.

The following sections are designed to provide tips and to help both instructors and students focus on higher-order learning activities.

3.2.1 Why Should We Write Detailed Syllabi?

In line with the authors' approach to teaching and learning T&I, the syllabi referred to in this section are process-oriented and therefore focus on preparatory tasks and post-performance reflections. They include activities such as researching subject-matter content and terminology, drafting and revising translations, drafting medical interpretation role-play, and reflecting on their translation and interpreting performances, to name but a few. While language teaching may call upon distinct syllabi that focus on either notional, situational, task-based, skill-based, or content-based frameworks, for example (Sabah 2018), we believe that these granular distinctions make less sense in the T&I classroom, where syllabi usually include a mix of such structures.

A highly detailed syllabus (based on the inclusive design framework, as discussed in Chapter 1) may incorporate items such as the following:

- an introduction by the instructor highlighting relevant aspects of their background for the particular course at hand
- course description and learning objectives
- housekeeping aspects such as ways to contact their instructor, instructor availability, and expected response time, as well as file naming and file format conventions
- support for online learning, including contact information for 24/7 tech support and online tutorials
- weekly schedule of readings, discussions, assignments, quizzes, and exams
- detailed list of readings and detailed description of assignments
- submission deadlines, grading policy, breakdown, and scale
- important statements, including statements on disability, diversity, academic honesty, and the use of machine translation tools, for instance

A clickable table of contents with a list of questions as shown in Figure 3.1 helps maximize student engagement. This list of questions is not too dissimilar from well-designed instructions manuals for household appliances ("What should I do if my microwave stops heating food?"). This approach anticipates the types of questions that students would typically ask in a classroom. Anticipation is a critical component of online learning in general and of syllabus design in particular. Instructors anticipating as many questions and issues as possible make for a more satisfying learning experience

Contents	
WHO AM I?	2
HOW TO CONTACT ME AND WHAT ARE MY OFFICE HOURS?	2
WHAT IS THIS COURSE ABOUT?	2
WHAT ARE THE COURSE OBJECTIVES?	2
WHAT ARE THE COURSE READINGS?	2
WHAT WILL YOU BE DOING WEEK BY WEEK?	3
SUMMARY OF ASSIGNMENTS OTHER THAN VOICETHREAD DISCUSSIONS	5
FILE NAMING, SUBMISSIONS, AND DEADLINES	6
GRADE POLICY AND BREAKDOWN	6
GRADING SCALE	7
HOW WILL YOU PARTICIPATE IN ONLINE DISCUSSIONS?	7
HOW SHOULD YOU SUBMIT YOUR RECORDED INTERPRETING ASSIGNMENTS?	7
WHAT IF YOU NEED SUPPORT WITH WRITING YOUR PAPERS?	7
WHAT IF YOU NEED TECH SUPPORT WITH BLACKBOARD?	7
WHAT IS A RUBRIC AND HOW CAN IT HELP YOU WITH YOUR ASSIGNMENTS?	7
A FEW TIPS ABOUT ONLINE LEARNING	7
ATTENDANCE POLICY	7
WHAT EMAIL ADDRESS SHOULD YOU USE?	8
PLEASE READ CAREFULLY! ACADEMIC HONESTY POLICY STATEMENT	8
DISABILITY STATEMENT	8

Figure 3.1 Syllabus Table of Contents

for students and a smoother teaching experience for themselves, including saving time. The authors speak from their own experience teaching online and sometimes learning the hard way.

Instructors who indicate their usual response time (i.e., "The instructor will respond to students' emails within 24 hours from Monday to Friday") will avoid creating false expectations (i.e., students expecting to receive a response within an hour on a Sunday morning) and frustrations on both ends. Furthermore, the online environment sometimes creates the illusion of instantaneous and permanent availability from the instructor, akin to the 24/7 technical support offered by most LMSs. Anticipation also requires being as specific as possible. Incorporating into the syllabus what might seem like mundane details at first, such as file naming instructions, alleviates the instructor's burden, such as having to deal with 25 files identically named "Translation" instead of "Week1_Translation_Janet_Johnson," which is a very frustrating experience for any instructor reviewing student assignments or for instructors teaching multilingual or language-neutral courses, who have to sort through assignments before sending them to language-specific reviewers (the concept of language reviewing in multilingual classes is further discussed in Chapter 5). Moreover, teaching file naming conventions helps translation learners achieve professional verisimilitude. As pre-professionals, students need to understand the necessity of file-naming consistency and to put themselves in the shoes of the file receiver(s). Such information can also be offered and reinforced to students in different ways, such as through recorded tutorials uploaded to the LMS or webpages of certain programs.

3.2.2 Why Should We Repeat Instructions in Different Places?

As mentioned previously, some instructions or specifications indicated on the course syllabus will need to be repeated, probably in an expanded form, in various locations within the course LMS itself. Envisioning these repetitions as an echo to what is normally stated (reasonably expected from instructors at the college level) in the classroom is quite helpful. For instance, it is reasonable to give a short description of online discussion guidelines in the syllabus so that students know what to expect when reading the document. These guidelines may be repeated in the course LMS itself, should the instructor decide to introduce each type of activity or assignment on the course's home page for instance. The guidelines will be repeated, albeit in an expanded form, in each weekly discussion assignment description in the course LMS to avoid requiring students to constantly navigate between multiple screens or go back to refer to earlier modules. As discussed previously, designing the entire syllabus upfront might be the best approach to avoid losing time editing descriptions or instructions. However, back and forth adjustments between the course syllabus and the course LMS are hardly avoidable.

3.2.3 Should We Give Syllabus Quizzes?

Short, lower-stake open-book quizzes in the online environment encourage students to engage with the content at hand, starting with the syllabus. Designing a short quiz to make sure students have read and understood critical components of the syllabus will save students and instructors alike a good amount of time later in the semester (one of the authors has experimented with online teaching without syllabus quizzes at first and will not go back to making that costly mistake). Open-ended questions combined with multiple-choice ones are also an easy way for the instructor to get an immediate sense of their students' individual strengths and challenges. Quizzes may include questions on the specific learning objectives of the course, the types of assignments, the weight of discussions in their overall grade, file naming conventions, technology needed for a specific interpretation assignment, or the date of the final exam, and may elicit immediate questions from some students. This tool helps students engage closely with the syllabus content and advantageously replaces the review of the syllabus that usually takes place in face-to-face classes. These lower-stake quizzes need to be set up as graded items; otherwise, some students will consider them optional and not take them.

3.2.4 Should We Use Screenshots?

Inserting screenshots into syllabi as illustrated with the title and icon of **Course Materials/Course Reserve** in Figure 3.2 will, for instance, reduce the flow of early weeks emails regarding the location of the course readings in the LMS.

Similarly, to help students easily navigate between the course syllabus and course LMS, instructors may also include screenshots of the syllabus in the course LMS itself as shown with the "**Content of week 1**" section in the screenshot from a Blackboard course page in Figure 3.3.

For the sake of accessibility and as a word of caution, any image added to a document or to an online platform should be described for students who need extra support, such as those who are visually impaired. Most LMSs today incorporate accessibility check when instructors are building their

WHAT ARE THE COURSE READINGS?
All required readings and materials are subject to change and will be posted on Blackboard under Course Materials/Course Reserve, which looks like this on Blackboard (copied in many places on Blackboard, including in Reading and Discussion folders):

Figure 3.2 Screenshot of LMS Course Shell Excerpt in Syllabi

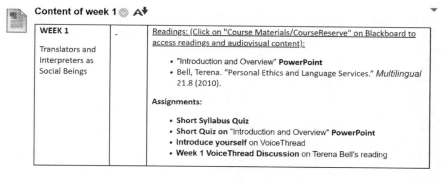

Figure 3.3 Screenshot of Syllabi Excerpts in LMS Course Shell

course's content. Images will then be read by software such as Read&Write or others.

3.3 Designing Learning Outcomes

In a conference presentation, John Hollenbeck (2020) points out that traditional learning outcomes use verbs that are not measurable, such as "understand," "appreciate" (which relies on emotions), or "know," to name but a few. Anderson and Krathwohl's (2001) revision of the original Bloom's taxonomy (Bloom and Krathwohl 1956) points to a more dynamic approach to learning, and lists verbs such as "explain," "describe," "categorize," "perform," "analyze," "produce," or "create." When designing their syllabi, instructors should strive for a balance of higher-order thinking skills and lower-order ones and keep in mind that lower-order ones, albeit necessary, are not sufficient alone. The authors discuss this balance in greater detail in Chapter 5, in the section addressing learning outcomes.

Hollenbeck suggests envisioning learning objectives as statements describing what students will be able to do after taking a course. Course descriptions should include the performance learners are expected to achieve, and describe it with specific and measurable learning outcomes, where "specific" and "measurable" are first and foremost understood from the learner's perspective. Course descriptions should include specific learning objectives stating what students will or should be able to do, provide examples of assessments as evidence of achievement, specify instructional materials and technologies that students need to perform a task, and indicate the type of activities students will do to practice. When instructors list the series of "things" that they expect their students to be able to do at the end of the course, they should include a description of the tools students are allowed to use or not use, the conditions or context of execution, and the real-world conditions a specific task or performance takes place in (Hollenbeck 2020). Quantitative criteria can be added as needed.

Let us apply these principles to a multilingual Introduction to Interpretation course. In the example that follows, the "perform sight translation" learning objective is tied to an assignment description and is used to identify elements of Hollenbeck's learning design mapping, including the **performance** itself, the **context**, the **conditions**, and the **quantitative** criteria: "Perform a one-page sight translation from English into the student's LOTE (language other than English) in a community interpretation setting with prior topic preparation. The task will be performed using XYZ video capture program and recorded with the camera on."

The performance itself is a **sight translation**, the context is a **community interpretation setting** (health care, education, or public service, for instance), the conditions are the **use of a video capture program with the camera on** (to make sure the student is actually performing a sight translation without any visual aid), and the quantitative criteria is the **length of the document** to be sight translated ("one page").

Criteria can point to any type of quantifiable elements, such as duration, speed, number of words, number of pages, etc. In a simultaneous interpretation task, this could be expressed as "perform simultaneous interpretation of a **120-word-per-minute** speech for **10 minutes**," where criteria of both speed and length are provided. In a translation task, instructors can define various criteria such as the number of words, the amount of time allowed to accomplish the task (as an indication of professional environment speed), or the number of reliable external resources used to research terminology and verify the use of the terms in context.

Table 3.1 Illustration of Learning Design Mapping

Learning Objective	Assessment	Instructional Materials	Learner Activity and Interaction	Technologies
What learners should be able to do	Evidence	Using	Practice	

Source: Hollenbeck (2020)

Learning design mapping tables are helpful instruments for instructors writing learning outcomes and even designing their entire syllabus since such tables help instructors to visualize the links between various elements that weigh on structuring course materials and writing assignment descriptions. Table 3.1 illustrates Hollenbeck's model (2020):

Four or five learning outcomes per course are usually sufficient, suggests Hollenbeck, as each learning objective should equate a substantial amount of work for learners. An useful exercise for T&I instructors is to examine an existing syllabus with its learning objectives and try to map them with Hollenbeck's model described previously.

3.4 Selecting an LMS

"The attractiveness of online learning via LMSs is associated with the promise of providing access to a diverse set of constructive pedagogies" (Gillani, quoted in Demmans Epp et al. 2020, 3264). Constructivists have pointed out that LMSs allow students to access a wide selection of resources and materials and allow for student interactions, which make course content more digestible through the individual curation of said content by diverse students (Demmans Epp et al. 2020).

Choosing an LMS is an important consideration, but it is oftentimes outside the instructors' purview, as these choices are usually made at the institutional level. However, understanding how different LMSs can impact students' learning experiences and behaviors is important, especially for those instructors who have their say in selecting a system and want the selected LMS to support their particular learning goals. For instance, Demmans Epp et al. (2020) point out that threaded discussions and their visual layouts may impact how learners interact.

Blackboard, Moodle, and Coursera, to name but a few, all seem to promote an instructivist paradigm, in which instructors provide learners with knowledge (Demmans Epp et al. 2020). A large-scale study showed that Blackboard's own content delivery tools are, for instance, heavily transmission-based, accounting for more than 75% of student activities (Whitmer et al. 2016). However, other tools can be integrated into Blackboard that promote a different, constructivist approach. One of such collaborative tools, and one that is particularly suitable for interpretation assignments, is VoiceThread, introduced in Section 3.5.3. In 2021, students of one of the authors inquired toward the end semester about the possibility of a social interaction space that could be built into the course LMS, whose design and built-in features did not provide such a space. The lack of *social* interactions, as opposed to *academic* discussions, was perceived as isolating and preventing students from benefitting from a full learning experience.

Other LMSs, such as Pepper, were designed with a social constructivism framework in mind and might be a better choice for instructors looking for a platform that has built-in features promoting social interaction and collaboration, rather than focusing on the consumption of instructor-provided content (Demmans Epp et al. 2020).

Regardless of the type of LMS chosen for delivering the course, instructors act as managers of the course shell. They can add tools to compensate for lacking features, as discussed previously, and have options in terms of organizing its content. The screenshots shown in Figures 3.4, 3.5, and 3.6 illustrate the visual architecture of weekly modules and their subfolders in Blackboard and caveats associated with the student view vs. what instructors see.

As shown in the last two screenshots (Figures 3.5 and 3.6), students do not see the same architecture as instructors. Instructors have the option to select Student View, but students do not have the option to select Instructor View. This example illustrates the need, with certain LMSs, for instructors to constantly put themselves in their students' shoes and check that students indeed see and have access to what instructors share in the course shell.

However, it is important to state that the instructor's role is not to offer technical help. This needs to be very clearly and repeatedly communicated to students throughout the semester. Students often forget that they can

Figure 3.4 Shared Instructor and Student View of Weekly Modules on Blackboard

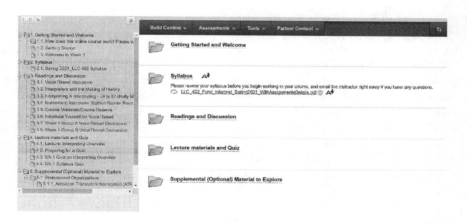

Figure 3.5 Instructor View of Subfolders Inside Week 1 Module

contact the LMS's helpdesk for technical support—usually via chat, telephone, or email. When confronted with an issue, our natural impulse as human beings is to turn to a person we know. It is therefore perfectly normal for students to spontaneously contact their instructor, with whom

58 Online Course Development

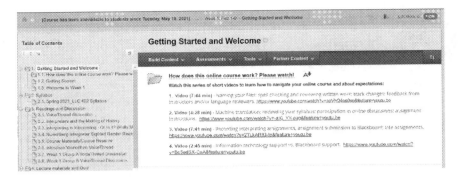

Figure 3.6 Student View of Subfolders Inside Week 1 Module

they have developed a relationship, with any technical issue they encounter. As a consequence, it is helpful to provide a few examples of issues for which students should contact the helpdesk in the syllabus, maybe include this question on the syllabus quiz, and to let them know about the helpdesk availability (larger institutions usually provide 24/7 LMS support, while others may offer limited availability).

3.5 Building Other Digital Tools into the Course Design

Integrating other digital tools, especially collaborative tools, into the LMS chosen for delivering the course is particularly important in light of the potential design biases discussed previously (i.e., instructivist vs. constructivist designs). Collaborative tools can be added to compensate for the instructivist bias inherent to many LMSs. These tools may include VoiceThread, Padlet, Discord, and Google Docs, to name just a few. Other tools such as screen capture software, when this feature is not already integrated into the LMS, allow instructors to record lectures, for instance, slides with audio-recorded comments. These digital tools and technologies aim not only to replicate or replace what could happen in the classroom but to *enhance* student learning. In the following section, we will discuss a few of these tools and how they can be applied in the online T&I classroom.

3.5.1 Video Capture

Screen recorders, also called video capture software, record what happens on the screen as if a video camera were pointed at it while recording one's voice. It is useful to look up the latest reviews of screen recorders such as Baxter's (2021, n. pag.) when selecting a tool. Screen recorders are a powerful way to personalize instruction. From the students' perspective, video captures are "almost like having [their] personal tutor whose message never changes regardless of how many times [they] rewind or review the content. Anytime, anyplace, on demand instruction" (Yearwood interviewed by Kelly 2011).

Avoiding jargon or complicated terms when they have not been introduced is an important factor when creating lecture recordings, since students do not have the option to interact with the instructor as in a face-to-face or synchronous environment. Everyday language and simple explanations are likely to have a better impact on students from various backgrounds, especially in multilingual courses.

Another important consideration when planning to incorporate videos into our online courses is length. A large-scale study by the Massachusetts Institute of Technology (MIT) in 2014 recommended that videos be shorter than 6 minutes. Their research also found out that "videos that intersperse an instructor's talking head with slides are more engaging than slides alone," and that online course videos recorded by instructors with high enthusiasm are more engaging (Guo, Kim, and Rubin 2014, 2). Another study, by researchers from the University of Wisconsin-Stout with 154 students concluded that "a majority of students believed the videos helped them learn course content and that the videos were best kept to less than 15 minutes in length" (Berg et al. 2014, 1). Whatever short length instructors decide to adopt, the same advice regarding accessibility should be followed. Instructors' videos should have the option of offering closed captioning for deaf or hard-of-hearing students. And there is nothing wrong with surveying our own students to use their feedback in terms of length.

Common applications include Camtasia, Screencast-O-Matic, Echo 360, as well as many others. Some of them are already built into specific LMSs. Figure 3.7 shows an example of a short introductory lecture capture on Echo 360, which is integrated into Blackboard.

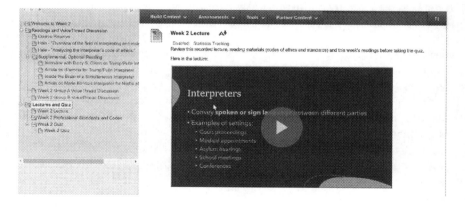

Figure 3.7 Student View of Recorded Lecture Using Echo 360 Screen Capture

3.5.2 Sample Uses of Video Capture Technologies in the Online T&I Classroom

Tutorial and Demonstrations

Ideal for introducing any T&I technology, showing a sequence of activities, such as:

- tutorials for CAT Tools
- tutorials for remote simultaneous interpreting (RSI) platforms
- demonstration of operations, for instance terminology research, showing the various steps in the process

Student Assignments

Students can advantageously use these technologies themselves to demonstrate their mastery of the functionalities of specific tools such as RSI platforms, CAT Tools, terminology management tools such as term extraction, bilingual concordancers, or document alignment. In turn, a selection of video capture recorded by students themselves can be showcased as exemplars in a later iteration of the course, provided they give permission to their instructor to do so.

Non-T&I-Specific Use of Video Captures:

- introduction to the syllabus
- instructions for submitting an assignment on the course LMS
- instructions for taking a test
- instructions for using tools that require a learning curve, such as Voice Thread

3.5.3 VoiceThread

This rich media content application can be integrated to LMS courses, which is the case at the institution where the authors work. It is designed to offer an alternative to text-only discussions and "fills the social presence gap associated with online courses"[1] since participants can choose between written, audio recorded, and video recorded comments. These multisensory options greatly enhance student motivation and social presence and make for lively student interactions.

VoiceThread can be used in reading discussions, recorded lectures (for instance to elicit student comments and participation), and assignments. It is particularly suitable for all three modes of interpretation assignments: sight translation, consecutive interpretation, and simultaneous interpretation. Audio or video exemplars can be uploaded by the instructor to a Voice Thread-designated space where students upload their own recordings, access their peers' recordings, and provide feedback on them. Written, audio, or video comments can be inserted into any point in a video. This video provided by VoiceThread and mentioned earlier illustrates the benefits of such a tool; instructors can easily imagine how it can benefit students in an online interpretation classroom: see note 1.

3.5.4 Padlet

Padlet is an online virtual bulletin board, where students can collaborate, reflect, and share resources in one specific and secure location accessible with a custom URL created by their instructor. This collaborative tool allows learners to post anonymously and instructors to moderate posts. It is a web-based board that does not require any software installation. It is very user-friendly and does not require any instructions. Padlet can be used for collaborative note-taking, brainstorming, for collecting suggestions or eliciting whiteboard answers, or for gathering research resources.

3.5.5 Quizlet

Web-based study application Quizlet is a useful tool for simple glossary building or reviewing terminology before an interpretation assignment, for example. It allows users to create their own flashcards, use others' flashcards when people make them publicly accessible, and study them using various games and self-testing.

3.5.6 Discord

Discord is a discussion and collaboration tool for creating topic-based text channels as well as voice and video conversations, screen sharing, and podcasting.

The tools and ideas discussed in this chapter are only suggestions to create meaningful interactions between all actors in the classroom. They help foster horizontal interactions rather than vertical, top-down ones. Within a given course, overlap between the LMS course shell and the syllabus is desirable and akin to instructors repeating instructions or information in multiple ways in a face-to-face classroom (on the board, orally, at the beginning and end of class, etc.). Chapter 4 will build on the self-directed and intentional learning framework discussed in this chapter and examine the role(s) and presence of the instructor in an online environment.

Note

1 https://voicethread.com/products/highered/.

References

Anderson, Lorin, and David Krathwohl, editors. *A Taxonomy for Learning, Teaching, and Assessing: A Revision of Blooms Taxonomy of Educational Objectives*. Longman, 2001.

Baxter, Baril. "The Best Free Screen Recorders in 2021." *Techradar*, 28 June 2021, www.techradar.com/news/the-best-free-screen-recorder.

Berg, Richard, et al. "Leveraging Recorded Mini Lectures to Increase Student Learning." *The Teaching Professor*, 1 Feb. 2014, www.teachingprofessor.com/topics/teaching-strategies/teaching-with-technology/leveraging_recorded_mini_lectures_to_increase_student_learning/.

Blinne, Kristen C. "Start with the Syllabus: HELPing Learners Learn Through Class Content Collaboration." *College Teaching*, vol. 61, no. 2, Apr. 2013, pp. 41–3.

Bloom, Benjamin S., and David R. Krathwohl. *Taxonomy of Educational Objectives: The Classification of Educational Goals* (First edition). Longmans, Green, 1956.

Campbell, S. "Towards a Model of Translation Competence." *Meta*, vol. 36, no. 2–3, 1991, pp. 329–43.

Darby, Flower. *Small Teaching Online: Applying Learning Science in Online Classes*. Wiley, 2019.

Demmans Epp, C., et al. "Learning Management System and Course Influences on Student Actions and Learning Experiences." *Education Tech Research and Development*, vol. 68, 2020, pp. 3263–97.

Guo, Philip J., et al. "How Video Production Affects Student Engagement: An Empirical Study of MOOC Videos." *Proceedings of the First ACM Conference on Learning at Scale*, 2014, pp. 41–50, http://up.csail.mit.edu/other-pubs/las2014-pguo-engagement.pdf.

Hollenbeck, John. *Begin Here: Creating Effective Learning Objectives*. OLC—Online Learning Consortium, 2020, https://onlinelearningconsortium.org/olc-innovate-2020-session-page/?session=8498&kwds=hollenbeck.

Jafar, Afshan. "Student Engagement, Accountability, and Empowerment: A Case Study of Collaborative Course Design." *Teaching Sociology*, vol. 44, no. 3, 2016.

Kelly, Rob. "Using Screen Capture Software to Improve Student Learning." *Faculty Focus*, 15 Mar. 2011, www.facultyfocus.com/articles/teaching-with-technology-articles/using-screen-capture-software-to-improve-student-learning/.

Sabah, Salman Sabbah. "English Language Syllabuses: Definition, Types, Design, and Selection." *Arab World English Journal*, vol. 9, no. 2, 2018, pp. 127–42.

Washbourne, Richard Kelly. "The Self-Directed Learner: Intentionality in Translator Training and Education." *Perspective Studies in Translatology*, vol. 22, no. 3, Oct. 2013, pp. 1–15.

Whitmer, J., et al. *Patterns in Blackboard Learn Tool Use: Five Course Design Archetypes*. Blackboard, 2016, www.blackboard.com/sites/default/files/resource/pdf/Bb_Patterns_LMS_Course_Design_r5_tcm135-42998.pdf.

Yee, Megan. "Why 'Safe Spaces' Are Important for Mental Health—Especially on College Campus." *Healthline*, n.d. www.healthline.com/health/mental-health/safe-spaces-college#2. Accessed 15 June 2021.

4 Instructor Presence in Online Courses

Synchronous and Asynchronous Considerations

This chapter explores the rationale of online presence, introduces notions such as connectivism, builds on socio-constructivism, and guides instructors on various tools to implement it. It provides examples of feedback on language-specific and non-language-specific assignments, sample Echo 360 universal capture lectures, and VoiceThread multimodal discussion audio comments.

It is important to start this chapter with a disclaimer. Striking the right balance for online presence is an art rather than a science as finding the right dose of instructor presence and establishing the tone one wants to convey takes time and requires experimenting with different tools and approaches. Notwithstanding technology and connectivity issues pertaining to virtual meetings, establishing one's tone in synchronous online classes is more straightforward than in asynchronous classes, since synchronous classes take place live, albeit mediated by a screen. In asynchronous classes, instructors will convey their personal tone and approach to teaching via a variety of communication channels (written, audio, or video channels), and using various types of communications (feedback on assignments, class announcements, individual emails, lecture videos, etc.). However, taking a step back, one must argue that instructor presence in online courses actually starts in the instructional design phase and the production of content and a syllabus. In regular in-person classrooms, students take class preparation and planning for granted because they can interact with their teachers in the offline environment and clarify any questions they might have. In remote learning, their first contact with instructors is through reviewing course syllabi and content delivery design.

The timeliness and frequency of instructor-student communications are also key elements in asynchronous settings. The authors believe that calling upon all three types of communication channels allows instructors to leverage three cornerstones of human relationships: I see you, I hear you, I respond to you. In turn, this multichannel online presence, together with content selection and instructional delivery design, can be leveraged by students to establish their own presence and to communicate with their

DOI: 10.4324/9781003149316-5

classmates and instructors using the full spectrum of communication channels and preferred literacies (written, audio, and/or video).

In the first section of this chapter, we address the topic of digital literacy. As alluded to in Chapter 1, multilingual online translation and interpreting classes in general attract different student populations, with different educational, socioeconomic, and geographic backgrounds. Therefore, online learning literacies should be at the forefront of the debate on equity.

4.1 How Can Instructors Address the Range of Digital Literacies Among Students?

As already mentioned, instructors teaching online will encounter a wider range of student backgrounds than in face-to-face settings. Some students have poor bandwidth or Internet connections, or limited access to a computer (for instance, one device shared by multiple family members), and/or difficulty accessing a quiet environment, which may pose an issue for audio- or video-recorded assignments. Other students, depending on their personal background, may also have limited computer skills. Let us not forget that community interpreters did not, until the pandemic, need advanced computer skills. The pandemic compelled many community interpreters around the world to switch overnight to computer-mediated interpretation, which involved the many technological issues that come with such a move that do not only relate to their computer literacy and technology levels. For example, in a recent webinar at the University of Massachusetts Amherst, Vonessa Costa, Director of Multicultural Affairs & Patient Services at Cambridge Health Alliance, shared some of the lessons learned during COVID-19 pandemic in her hospital system, when most of their staff had to pivot to remote interpreting. Costa recalls that they realized only much later into the pandemic, when technical and connection issues were happening, that they were asking the wrong questions before sending their health care interpreters to work from home. Her advice to institutions thinking about a work-from-home scenario is to start with questions such as "how much broadband do you have?", "how many people use the same connection at home and for what purpose (gaming, remote learning, working from home)?", and "what is happening in your neighborhood in terms of latency (service provider variation, record numbers of people working and learning from home, brownouts/blackouts)?" (Costa 2020). While students signing up for online community interpretation classes may not need advanced computer skills to work and perform as in-person community interpreters, basic digital literacy is a requirement to take online classes (see the seven elements of digital literacies in Figure 4.1).

The San Diego Foundation (thereafter TSDF) defines the digital divide as encompassing "the ability, both technical and financial, to make full use of the technology available, taking into consideration access, or lack of access, to the internet" (TSDF 2020). In an earlier attempt at a definition, Nielsen

Instructor Presence in Online Courses   65

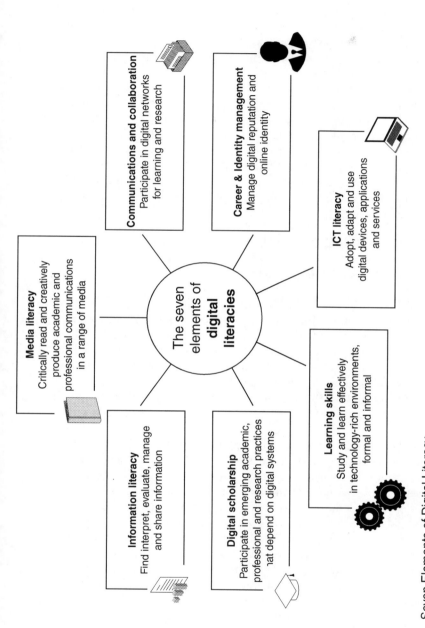

Seven Elements of Digital Literacy

Figure 4.1 JISC Digital Literacy Model
Source: Creative Commons

(2006, referred to in TSDF 2020) categorized the digital divide into three stages, namely the economic, usability, and empowerment divides. Today, "[t]he focus of the digital divide has shifted from access to computers and smartphones to inequity between those who have more or less bandwidth and more or less skills, also known as digital literacy" (TSDF 2020).

Low digital literacy among students taking an online course equates to students not being able to read fluently in an earlier, non-digital era. It is therefore crucial that institutions offering online courses provide technical support and tutorials to their student body, since technical support is outside of the purview of instructors. However, instructors need to be knowledgeable about the type of support offered by their institution and its availability. Such information needs to be clearly announced, first in the course syllabus, then repeated on the LMS course shell, as shown in the following guiding questions excerpted from a redacted syllabus. Such information can also be made available on the web pages of individual certificate programs and departments.

"WHAT IF YOU NEED TECH SUPPORT WITH [insert name of LMS]?
[Insert name of LMS] offers 24/7 online support via chat, email, or phone [insert URL to tech support information].

A FEW TIPS ABOUT ONLINE LEARNING
Students are encouraged to watch tutorials offered on the website of [insert name of institution] Continuing Education Division: [insert URL]
How to use [insert name of LMS]? Because this is an online class, students are expected to become familiar with [insert name of institution]'s online platform, [insert name of LMS]. Please seek help from [insert name of institution]'s IT support [insert URL] if you have any questions."

Additionally, instructors need to provide URLs to tutorials pertaining to specific tasks, such as taking a quiz, posting comments on a discussion thread, accessing grades, viewing assignments, giving and receiving feedback, etc. It is good practice to include information about all these tutorials in the introduction or welcome week on the LMS, and to repeat them again in each individual task. For instance, in the instructions to the first quiz of the semester, it is a good idea to include the URLs to tutorials explaining 1) how to take a quiz, 2) how to access grades, and 3) how to view their instructor's feedback. Depending on their teaching styles and student populations, instructors may want to repeat including these tutorials for each type of assignment over the first few weeks or throughout the semester. Building redundancy into the course materials is a good idea, e.g., for important deadlines, or for file naming or submission instructions.

Trite as it may sound, patience, availability, and flexibility are crucial in the first two weeks of any online course. During that time, some students might submit the wrong assignment to the platform. Depending on the class size and other considerations, offering to exceptionally accept them via email in case of such mishaps might be a good idea at the beginning, while reinforcing that all assignments need to be submitted to the LMS. Students taking their first online course might want to be reassured that their instructor can see their submissions and might email their instructors to verify that. Others will have trouble seeing the deadline of a given assignment. Based on the authors' own experiences, most students are over the learning curve after the second or third week in any given course. Some students will, however, need more support and guidance than others because of the lack of direct contact with their instructors. In the United States, for example, faculty members are expected to hold office hours for individual in-person meetings with students, which can be easily replicated in the remote environment. Offering short, one-on-one virtual meetings early on is important for those students, first to identify their specific challenges, then to suggest additional resources for them. One-one-one meetings also alleviate students' anxieties; talking live to their instructors makes them see the "real" human being, which is an important aspect for some students. It is important that instructors envision each of these early exchanges with students as an opportunity to reinforce expectations and encourage them to review the syllabus, online resources, and tutorials.

4.2 How Do Instructors Create and Maintain Online Presence in their Courses?

While online education is only a few decades old, with growing research and new theoretical frameworks underway, the community of inquiry (CoI) model developed by Garrison, Anderson, and Archer (1999) fits particularly well with our pedagogical framework (see Chapter 2). The CoI model envisions a collaborative and constructivist learning experience and relies on the interaction of three core elements: cognitive presence, teaching presence, and social presence, as shown in Figure 4.2.

Cognitive presence is the extent to which learners are able to construct and confirm meaning through sustained reflection and discourse (Garrison, Anderson, and Archer 2001). Teaching presence pertains to the "the design, facilitation, and direction of cognitive and social processes for the purpose of realizing personally meaningful and educationally worthwhile learning outcomes" (Anderson et al. 2001). Social presence refers to "the ability of participants to identify with the community (e.g., course of study), communicate purposefully in a trusting environment, and develop inter-personal relationships by way of projecting their individual personalities" (Garrison 2009).

In the following discussion, we provide illustrations of various ways of establishing our cognitive, teaching, and social presence as instructors, with the obvious overlap displayed on the CoI figure (see Figure 4.2).

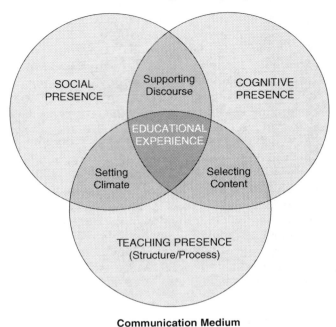

Figure 4.2 Community of Inquiry Model
Source: Garrison, Anderson, and Archer (1999, 88)

Recent research suggests including some synchronous (real-time) components to asynchronous courses as these might improve learning outcomes (Martin et al. 2020; Farros 2020). Other studies showed that synchronous online course orientations in asynchronous courses were directly linked to student success and retention (Fowler 2019). According to Yamagata-Lynch,

> synchronous online whole class meetings and well-structured small group meetings can help students feel a stronger sense of connection to their peers and instructor and stay engaged with course activities.
> (2014, 189–212)

Martin et al. coined the term "bichronous" to qualify online courses blending asynchronous and synchronous components,

> We define *bichronous online learning* as the blending of both asynchronous and synchronous online learning, where students can participate

in anytime, anywhere learning during the asynchronous parts of the course but then participate in real-time activities for the synchronous sessions. The amount of the online learning blend varies by the course and the activities included in the course.

(2020, n. pag.)

It is, however, important to keep in mind that students may choose fully asynchronous courses for specific reasons, including not having to attend any synchronous activity. Therefore, any synchronous component added to or embedded in an asynchronous course needs to be either fully optional (virtual office hours or one-on-one phone or video calls) or recorded and accessible in the form of a recording later (live webinars or presentations), unless the bichronous format is included in the course description ahead of time.

These synchronous components may take the form of one-on-one computer-mediated meetings as mentioned previously. Such individual meetings go a long way. They are necessary when instructors feel that back and forth emails are not helpful or are even counterproductive. Other synchronous components may include virtual office hours, offered at varied times for accrued flexibility due to various time zones and students' work and family commitments. Webinars with guest speakers represent an effective way to enhance online presence. Synchronous activities are not limited to the examples mentioned previously and can include other tools such as instant messaging, interactive whiteboards, or polling (Martin et al. 2020, n. pag.).

While the benefits of fully asynchronous courses can be subsumed as "anytime, anywhere," the challenges most often associated with the asynchronous modality include delays, lack of immediate feedback, and low levels of participation (Martin et al. 2020, n. pag.). Timely feedback and response to students' emails are therefore an important aspect in asynchronous courses and can be claimed as an integral part of instructor presence. However, as stated in Chapter 3, it is important to set specific expectations based on one's teaching style since a fully online environment might be associated with an illusion of permanent availability. Teaching online does not mean being always available nor does it require responding within an hour. Indicating one's usual response time (within 24 hours is a reasonable expectation for most instructors) and days of availability (maybe weekdays only) is important.

Low levels of participation have been identified as another frequent challenge associated with asynchronous courses. Not only can this be successfully addressed by designing lively asynchronous discussions in rich media content platforms, such as VoiceThread, but the authors even argue that students display greater deeper critical thinking skills in asynchronous discussions than in face-to-face classroom ones (Jay-Rayon, Langdon, & Mazzei 2020). Designing very specific rubrics for such discussions is key for reaching the desired outcomes (see Chapter 5 for a detailed discussion on rubrics), and for not only enhancing the instructor's teaching presence but also establishing students' cognitive and social presences, creating classroom dynamics with peer-to-peer responses, which is crucial in a socio-constructivist model of learning that challenges a top-down approach to teaching and learning.

Online students, especially non-traditional ones as discussed in Chapter 1, and to whom Costa refers to as "new-traditional" students (2020, 51; after Rendón 1994), also need to be validated. In 1994, Rendón analyzed the factors that helped these non- or new-traditional students succeed in higher education courses and found out that when a campus community member, be they faculty member, adviser, or other staff member, validated them, they were motivated to succeed. The social presence of the instructor therefore needs to include a form of validation, either addressed to the entire group in the form of a group message congratulating all students for the quality of their work on a particular assignment, a weekly wrap up highlighting specific achievements, snippets from their weekly reflections, or any other form of group validation. These small actions go a long way in establishing one's presence and reiterating the "I see you, I hear you, I respond to you," mentioned earlier, to which could be added, "I validate you." Individual validation might include a congratulatory email to a specific student, asking permission to use their anonymized work as an exemplar, or asking a particular student to share their experience with the entire class as an enrichment. The following is an illustration of this last category: A student in one of the authors' medical interpretation courses brought up, in one of their weekly discussion comments, their long experience dealing with non-professional interpreters (family members and friends) as a civil servant in a public service setting in the United States. The author identified this as a learning opportunity for all other students of that particular class, and offered that the student prepare a short, synchronous (and recorded) webinar on the topic, thus validating that particular student and recognizing their value as a source of learning for their peers. Such items can not only serve as learning objects (McGreal 2004) in future iterations of a given course, but can, if properly introduced as student-generated learning objects, also serve modeling goals for future students. Another example embracing that model is the 2020 Subtitling Box Festival (Mazzei 2020), which compiled the subtitling projects of the first cohort of an online audiovisual translation course that were then used for inspiration, modeling, and guidance by the next cohort. These are a few examples of inter-cohort learning across time. Other learning objects created by students can include self-evaluations, reflections, or glossaries, etc.

Instructor presence should therefore be pursued in different ways and should appeal to various senses. It is best envisioned as a permanent exploration and should be rooted in the careful observation of different literacies, sensitivities, cultures, and beliefs across our student populations. It is helpful to turn to Laura Rendón's *sentipensante* pedagogy to conclude this discussion on instructor presence.

> The word *sentipensante* comes from a combination of two Spanish words: *sentir*, which means to sense or feel, and *pensar*, to think. Galeano is taking the stance that rationality and intuition can exist in dynamic and complementary opposition. Our early ancestors all over the world recognized this epistemological position, but as consciousness evolved, Western philosophers assumed that intellectual training and rationality alone were key for understanding.
> (Rendón 2008, 131)

Pointing to Descartes and other thinkers, Rendón discusses how major achievements across the humanities and sciences were possible because people had "breakthrough insights in dreams, visions, intuitive flashes, and altered states of consciousness" (Heinberg 1998, 125, quoted in Rendón 2008, 132) and defines her *sentipensante* pedagogy as one rooted in "wholeness, harmony, social justice, and liberation." (Rendón 2008, 132). *Sentipensante* pedagogy implies that instructors engage their intellectual, social, emotional, and spiritual selves. While valuing scientific exploration, this pedagogy also recognizes the role of intuition, creativity, and the importance of shared construction of meaning (Rendón 2008, 135), which lies at the heart of translation and interpreting activities.

4.3 What is the Role of Pre-Recorded Videos?

Pre-recorded videos can be divided into several categories: lecture videos, tutorial or instruction videos, and purely presence videos, although *any* video represents an opportunity to reinforce instructor presence. Illustrations of each of these categories are provided later.

Pictorial superiority was proven a long time ago (a picture is worth a thousand words), but animated pictures are even more powerful and videos are gradually replacing or enhancing written lectures, instruction manuals, and recipe books. With the move toward video content, instructors need to be aware of the needs of blind or deaf students and of the technology that has been developed to enable accessibility of audio and/or visual components. In certain learning institutions and countries, this might already be a requirement, but not in every geographic area. Blackboard, for instance, has built-in notification systems that remind instructors of the need for audio-describing visual content or captioning sound content.

Karen Costa claims that video content is more likely to be recalled and that such content captures students' attention way more effectively than text alone (2000, 53). She also insists on the power of aesthetics in the perceived usability of video lectures. A visually appealing deck of slides is important in establishing trust and reassuring students that the content will be easy to navigate.

> Aesthetic-usability effect is a basic design principle that can help us understand why videos might be so effective in the online classroom. It maintains that our perception of how something looks (i.e., whether we find it pleasing to the eye) influences our perception of how easy (or difficult) it will be to use that item (Lidwell, Holden, and Butler 2003). If we perceive something to be aesthetically pleasing, we believe that it will be easy to use. If we perceive something as aesthetically displeasing, we think that it will be difficult to use.
>
> (Costa 2000, 57)

One of the authors was able to recently experience the aesthetic-usability principle in an assignment in which students were asked to write a comparative analysis of two different subtitling tools (software or online platform) in an Audiovisual Translation course. Many students wrote in their introduction that their trust or mistrust in the subtitling tool was built on the aesthetics and user-friendliness of the companies' websites. The following are three excerpts from their reflections, showing the impact of visual aspects (italics added for emphasis):

> My first impressions of the [name of tool] and [name of tool] subtitling programs were made as a result of the *visual* impact of their respective websites.
>
> (Student A)

> The programs were chosen primarily on *aesthetics*, because both websites look very contemporary and very *pleasing to the eye*. (Some of the other websites looked like they were stuck in the '90s, which doesn't give me *confidence* in the quality of a program, because it doesn't give the impression of a program that has kept up with the time).
>
> (Student B)

> When I entered their respective websites, I was immediately attracted to [name of tool]'s overall *design*. The site was very user-friendly and easy to navigate. To me, this is a *good sign* that the software will also be *easy to use* and navigate.
>
> (Student C)

4.3.1 Lecture Videos

Research shows that shorter lectures are more effective than longer ones. As briefly discussed in Chapter 3, some studies, such as the one conducted by the University of Wisconsin (Emporia State University 2018), recommend keeping their length under 15 minutes, while a large-scale study conducted by MIT suggests to not go over 6 minutes (Emporia State University 2018). One way to address these recommendations is to chunk larger lectures into shorter lecture segments, maybe corresponding to one important concept or skill set. For instance, instead of recording a 40-minute video lecture on note-taking for consecutive interpretation, instructors may consider breaking down the lecture into several, short video lectures each focusing on a sub-topic, for instance, one on short-term memory, one on chunking and units of meaning, and one on developing a personalized system of symbols, for instance.

Research also suggests that interspersing slides and whiteboards with a camera capture of the instructor's face is more effective than displaying a mere "talking head." (Emporia State University 2018). While some instructors will feel more comfortable than others capturing themselves talking during their video lectures, whiteboard applications allow instructors to handwrite and demonstrate specific skills, such as note-taking, or to annotate a rubric, instructions, or a glossary, to name but a few, to mimic and even enhance a classroom board experience. Using whiteboards in recorded lectures replicates face-to-face settings, and is a powerful way of enhancing the teaching presence of the instructor, and provides an opportunity for expert modeling, which supports authenticity in the classroom.

Additionally, Costa points to the specific role of instructional videos in student engagement and motivation:

> instructional videos showed a moderate correlation to students' knowledge acquisition but an "overwhelmingly positive" correlation with students' perceptions of course quality (Morris and Chikwa 2013, 25). Student satisfaction and course engagement levels increase with the use of instructor-generated videos (Draus, Curran, and Trempus 2014) and graduate students reported that videos improved their connection with their instructor (Martin, Wang, and Sadaf 2018). In a recent review, Michelle Pacansky-Brock (n.d.), a well-respected online educator known for her work on humanizing online learning, points to both videos and voice threads as an effective strategy to humanize our online courses. Finally, video was a commonly utilized teaching strategy in a recent survey of award-winning online faculty (Martin, Budhrani, Kumar, and Ritzhaupt 2019).
>
> (Costa 2020, 63)

While scripts might be helpful at the beginning, Costa debunks the myth of attaining perfection in recorded lectures and suggests that the most engaging video lectures are the ones that are more spontaneous, which presupposes making minor mistakes or mispronouncing a word and making peace with these. Beginning online instructors subscribe to the myth of perfection, re-recording themselves to exhaustion (Costa 2020, 104). In terms of slide design, lean slides with very few words are suggested by presentation

74 *Instructor Presence in Online Courses*

experts (Reynold 2012 in Costa 2020) as research shows that people do not listen as attentively while they are reading (Horvath 2014 in Costa 2020). Slides are not speaker's notes. Rather, slides with one single idea, little text, and engaging pictures are apparently the most effective ones in capturing students' attention (Reynold 2012 in Costa 2020, 119). Figures 4.3 and 4.4 demonstrate examples of effective and ineffective slide designs.

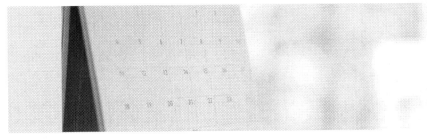

Figure 4.3 Model Slide

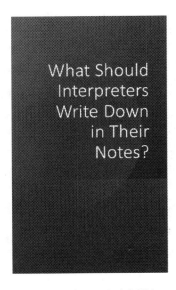

Figure 4.4 Anti-Model Slide

As can be surmised from the previous discussion and examples, lecture videos require a lot of time from instructors in the development phase or additional work and commitment afterward in the case of chunking a 60-minute recorded synchronous meeting or class into shorter 10-minute segments. In some cases, instructors can rely on the instructional design and technology departments and staff of their institutions, but in others, it is up to the teacher to take on video editing work without the expertise of graphic designers. One idea is to include students in the process, especially those with the skills necessary to compile and rearrange their instructors' videos into more manageable lengths.

4.3.2 Tutorial Videos (Screencasting)

Tutorial videos are of a different nature and might not include any slides at all. They are highly appreciated by students for demonstrating the use of new technologies or software, such as CAT Tools, terminology databanks, concordancers, subtitling programs, audio or video editing software, etc. Alternatively, such tutorials can advantageously be harvested from YouTube or other video-sharing platforms, as they allow instructors to not reinvent the wheel and invest their time in a wiser manner. Curating the content of a video tutorial by another author, in the form of introducing its content or pointing to specific elements in the video, for example, is also a good alternative for establishing one's teaching presence in tutorial videos.

4.3.3 Presence Videos

Purely presence videos are short videos that can be sent as announcements or posted as comments in discussion threads. These videos might combine information, encouragement, inquiring about the students' learning journeys, etc. When sent as an announcement, these short videos (sometimes less than 1 minute long) can be reinforced by a written message in the body of the announcement, such as in the example that follows. Students may watch the video while others will prefer to stick to the written message:

> Hello everyone, I hope this message finds you well. I hope you enjoyed the exercises on condensation and segmentation you just completed. I am confident you will feel much stronger as you tackle your first subtitling assignment this week. As we are moving toward Week 6, I would like to encourage each of you to check the content of that specific module since it is content-heavy. As always, do not hesitate to reach out to me if you have any questions or need clarifications. I am just an email away from Monday to Friday. Your discussion leaders for Week 5 are XXX and XXX (thank you, XXX and XXX!). Have a wonderful week.

Many institutions require a transcript for all audiovisual materials used in any given course. Automatic closed captions may also be activated by students, yet often yield disappointing results since AI relies on the quality of the audio and the speech, the elocution and accent of the speaker, among other elements that impede the results of automatically generated closed captions.

4.4 Instructor and Peer Feedback

Timely instructor feedback is crucial in online learning courses, and more specifically in asynchronous courses where feedback is one of the few occasions for students to have individualized interactions with their teachers. Detailed feedback represents the opportunity for students to learn from their mistakes and receive guidance in terms of research skills, methodology, and critical thinking. Since our approach to teaching and learning is rooted in socio-constructivism and based on processes and skill-building (see Chapter 2: Process-Oriented and Skill-Building Pedagogy), our idea of feedback is based on the same theoretical underpinning.

Washbourne's foundational publication on feedback in translator training (2014) provides an essential starting point to the discussion that follows,

> feedback potentially (1) models drafting as an iterative and recursive process; (2) prompts the translator to read his or her work as an interlocutor (a reader or user); (3) assists the learner via guided revision and builds capacity for self-directedness and self-assessment; (4) reinforces translating as a goal-oriented, strategic activity for different professional situations; (5) scaffolds a cognitively complex task; (6) promotes reflective practice; (7) is consistent with the field's movement away from instructionist practices; (8) adds a dimension of authenticity, as reception occurs outside the teacher–learner confines as well as within them; (9) engages the student with a problem-posing, collaborative format that respects the learner's emerging agency and encourages the democratization of the translation classroom; (10) harmonises with what is known about expertise acquisition, especially the role of feedback and corrective action in deliberate practice; and (11) provides opportunities for defending translation choices and using the metalanguage of the field to negotiate meaning.
>
> (Washbourne 2014, 240–1)

While encouraging self-inquiry and self-reflection should be at the forefront of any process-oriented pedagogy, it is important to distinguish different types of feedback, especially in multilingual classes. Non-language-specific feedback may include self-reflections on a translation or interpretation assignment in which students are asked to explain their challenges based on the specific rubric for the assignment, a comparative analysis of CAT tools or subtitling

Instructor Presence in Online Courses   77

tools, or a comparative analysis of dictionaries or terminology databanks. Such feedback should build self-directedness and focus on helping the students develop their research, documentation, and critical thinking skills. Feedback given on the self-evaluation of a translation or interpreting task, in which students are asked to critically analyze their strength and weaknesses, can be envisioned as a "feedback loop" (Washbourne 2014, 243) enabling students to monitor their performance, and to identify areas needing improvement and the means to do so. Additionally, and as alluded to and illustrated in Chapter 2, "[t]he give-and-take that emerges from individual feedback interactions can also be made group-wide" (Washbourne 2014, 243). The next two examples illustrate, in chronological order, individual feedback given on a self-reflection of a translation task (Figure 4.5), and a compilation of individual feedback interactions sent to the entire class (Table 4.1).

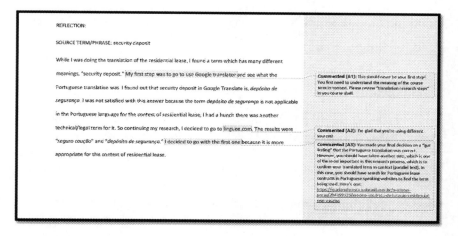

Figure 4.5 Sample Feedback on Self-Reflection of Translation Task

Table 4.1 Sample Compilation of Individual Feedback Interactions

General Feedback to all Students on Their Reflections of Using Translators' Forums
One word of advice: you need to do your own research first before posting a question, as discussed in the lecture. The forum should be the next step only if you can't find an appropriate target translation solution on your own. Professional translators don't like it when students have not done their "homework" first and they will call them on it.
Good work. I'm sorry you didn't get an answer to your question. Some of the reasons might be: 1) you didn't phrase your questions correctly. You need to indicate to translators in the forum that you have done your own research first. You need to provide context since words and terms cannot be understood without it; 2) they might not have found an answer because there is no target term in Vietnamese. Then you need to resort to some translation strategy: borrowing, calque, explanation, paraphrasing, reformulation, etc.

General Feedback to all Students on Their Reflections of Using Translators' Forums

I'm glad you got some good answers. However, one word of advice: do not ask questions that seem too easy (not a translation challenge) in these forums. You should only use the forums only after you have exhausted ALL your other resources (dictionaries, online searches, glossaries, etc.)

Posting a question such as "what is XXX?" in a translator's forum is not helpful to others. It also indicates you don't understand the importance of context. As a result, it's unlikely that you'll get any answers.

I'm glad you were able to get a response. As the responder indicated to you, someone had already posted the same question on Proz.com. So, before posting a question, look up the term in their "terminology search" tab first.

Good job! You posted clear questions and provided context! Don't forget to go back and THANK everyone for helping you. This is basic etiquette that needs to be followed in ALL these forums.

It seems you got some good answers from translators in the forum. This is a great resource if you know how to use it well. However, always remember that translators are not always 100% correct. It's always a good idea to include other steps in your research, such as confirming the target solution in parallel texts.

Language-specific feedback, as detailed and illustrated in the following examples, either by instructors who share the student's language pair, or external language reviewers hired in multilingual courses, should also encourage students to look for a solution by themselves (self-directness). Reviewers giving language-specific feedback might do the following:

- Point out similar subject-matter materials written in their target language, including relevant URLs and highlighting a relevant expression or passage, explain why the resource is a reliable one, and encourage the student to identify similarly reliable resources in their next assignment.
- Point out interferences within their language pair.
- Identify extra-linguistic references to help them solve a problem.
- Refer them to a more reliable or more specialized dictionary in their target language.
- Encourage them to use a spellchecker or editing software and suggest one (if available in their target language).
- Encourage them to take higher-level writing classes in their target language.

In the figures that follow (Figures 4.6.1, 4.6.2, 4.7.1, 4.7.2, and 4.7.3), we share some examples of feedback given in online translation and interpreting classes that illustrates the categories suggested previously, in the form of specific comments, advice, and suggestions, followed by general feedback pertaining to the student performance as a whole.

Instructor Presence in Online Courses 79

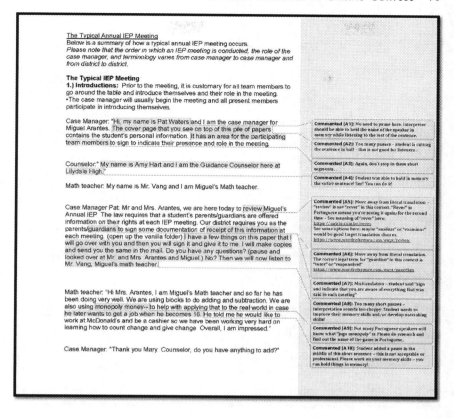

Figure 4.6.1 Sample Interpretation Assignment Feedback Using a Role-Play Script

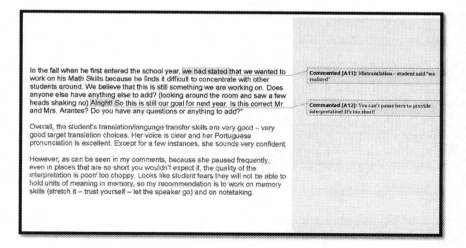

Figure 4.6.2 Sample Interpretation Assignment Feedback Using a Role-Play Script (cont.)

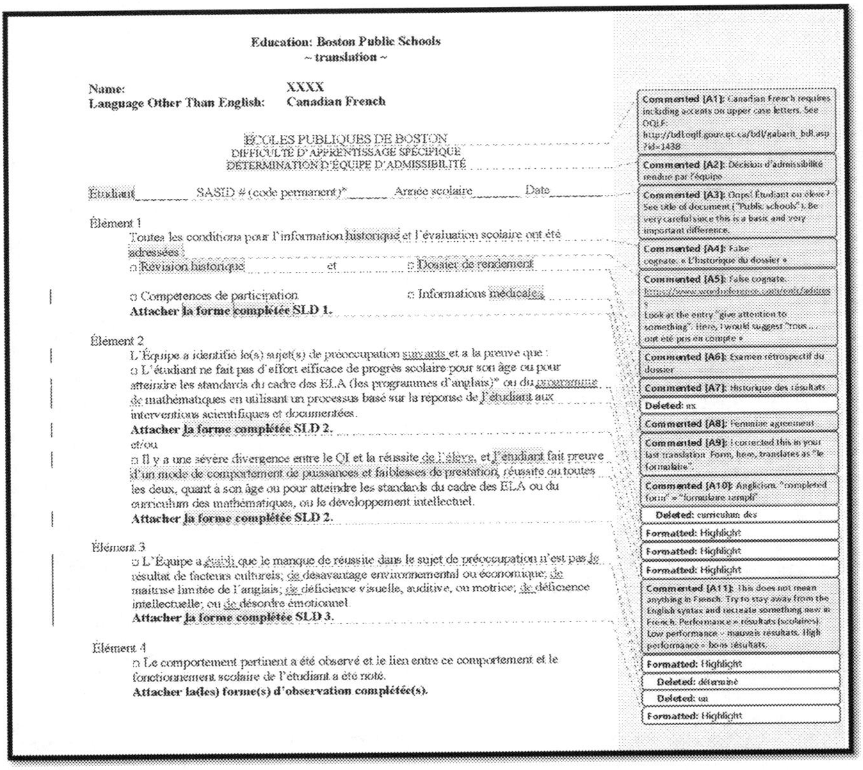

80 *Instructor Presence in Online Courses*

Figure 4.7.1 Sample Translation Assignment Feedback

In keeping with best practices for providing feedback, instructors should aim for a balance between corrective feedback and encouragement, especially at the early stage, at the beginning of the semester, or in fundamentals courses. Associating feedback with fault-finding is unfortunate, as feedback should be a means to reinforce learning in a positive way, thus acknowledging good finds, creativity, professionalism, attention to details, etc. Assuming that high-performing students, or students who mastered a task particularly well, know when and where they performed well is a mistaken position. Rather, instructors need to make a point of highlighting these positive elements to help students gradually recognize them by themselves.

Another form of feedback is that given by a peer. Peer-to-peer feedback is a multipronged learning opportunity: first, for the student receiving feedback, and second for the student or students giving some. One informal but

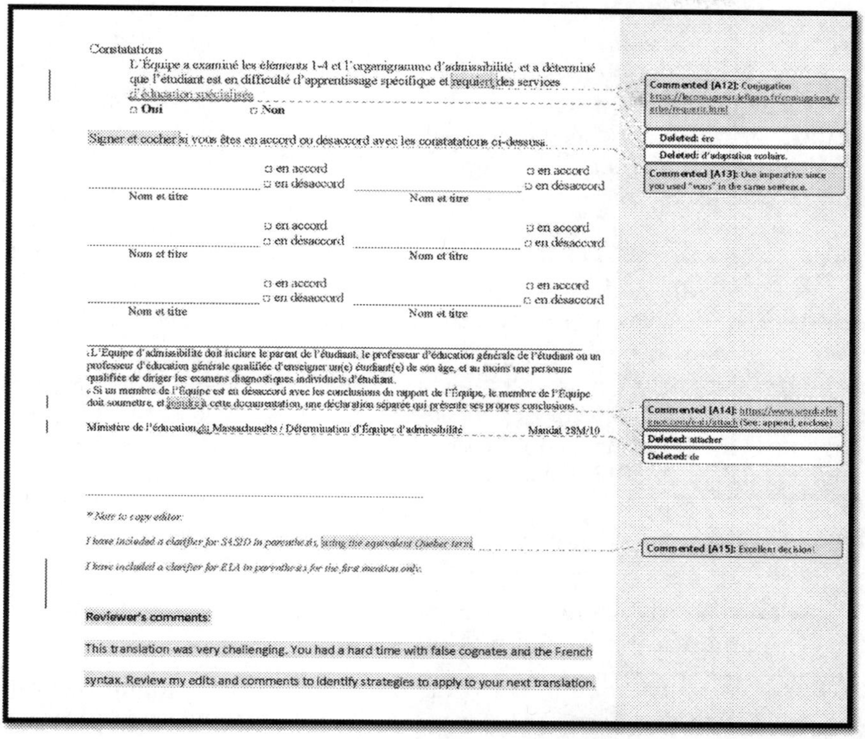

Constatations

L'Équipe a examiné les éléments 1-4 et l'organigramme d'admissibilité, et a déterminé que l'étudiant est en difficulté d'apprentissage spécifique et requiert des services d'éducation spécialisée

□ **Oui** □ **Non**

Signer et cocher si vous êtes en accord ou désaccord avec les constatations ci-dessus.

Nom et titre	□ en accord □ en désaccord	Nom et titre	□ en accord □ en désaccord
Nom et titre	□ en accord □ en désaccord	Nom et titre	□ en accord □ en désaccord
Nom et titre	□ en accord □ en désaccord	Nom et titre	□ en accord □ en désaccord

L'Équipe d'admissibilité doit inclure le parent de l'étudiant, le professeur d'éducation générale de l'étudiant ou un professeur d'éducation générale qualifiée d'enseigner un(e) étudiant(e) de son âge, et au moins une personne qualifiée de diriger les examens diagnostiques individuels d'étudiant.

Si un membre de l'Équipe est en désaccord avec les conclusions du rapport de l'Équipe, le membre de l'Équipe doit soumettre, et joindre à cette documentation, une déclaration séparée qui présente ses propres conclusions.

Ministère de l'éducation du Massachusetts / Détermination d'Équipe d'admissibilité Mandat 28M/10

** Note to copy editor:*

I have included a clarifier for SASID in parenthesis, using the equivalent Quebec term.

I have included a clarifier for ELA in parenthesis for the first mention only.

Reviewer's comments:

This translation was very challenging. You had a hard time with false cognates and the French syntax. Review my edits and comments to identify strategies to apply to your next translation.

Commented [A12]: Conjugation https://leconjugueur.lefigaro.fr/conjugaison/verbe/requerir.html

Deleted: ère

Deleted: d'adaptation scolaire.

Commented [A13]: Use imperative since you used "vous" in the same sentence.

Commented [A14]: https://www.wordreference.com/enfr/attach (See: append, enclose)

Deleted: attacher

Deleted: de

Commented [A15]: Excellent decision!

Figure 4.7.2 Sample Translation Assignment Feedback (cont.)

I suggest you review materials published in Quebec on a similar topic *before* engaging with the translation (examples include http://www.education.gouv.qc.ca/fileadmin/site_web/documents/dpse/evaluation/13-4602.pdf) as this approach has proven to be very effective in producing highly idiomatic translations.

Figure 4.7.3 Sample Translation Assignment Feedback (cont.)

effective way to encourage peer-to-peer feedback in non-language-specific settings is to design submissions in discussion forum settings, which means that all students can access their peers' assignments and comment on them once they have submitted their own. Based on our own students' comments in a range of courses where this setting has been experimented with, this method provides enrichment and represents a formidable improvement opportunity for learners. Students whose skills are lacking can access a range of authentic exemplars from their own cohort and are, in turn, motivated to develop their own skills. In multilingual courses, this might not always be possible for all language pairs, but some solutions include pairing the student with another student in a different class in the same country or overseas. The same settings can be applied in language-specific courses: Students submit their assignment first (recording of an interpreting assignment, translation, or glossary, for instance) and can learn from their peers in terms of translation choices, rephrasing, source of references, etc., and also provide their own feedback in the discussion thread. More formal feedback can be designed as a full-fledged activity, for instance to build revision skills. Designing a variety of peer-to-peer feedback activities participates in the non-vertical learning approach mentioned earlier.

4.5 A Few Words About the Do's and Don'ts of Communication in Online Courses

Mediated communication in the virtual environment refers to any form of communication that does not happen face-to-face. It is important to reflect on the type of channel that is appropriate to what we want to communicate. Synchronous video communications come closest to what happens in face-to-face settings and include non-verbal cues and body language. Video calls using videoconferencing platforms such as Zoom, Skype, or LMS-embedded tools are examples of synchronous communications, while pre-recorded videos as discussed previously are asynchronous and unidirectional. Audio communications at least include tone, which is an important verbal cue, to convey mood or emotions beyond our choice of words. Tone can be heard on voice mail or audio-recorded comments (asynchronous communications), or on phone calls (synchronous communications). Written communications, including emails, announcements, written instructions, and content on the LMSs, will automatically exclude any non-verbal cues and body language.

Social media has greatly changed the perception of what is acceptable or not in terms of communication in an academic setting. Some younger generation students in the Western world sometimes miss what communication etiquette implies in a course setting (such as including a greeting in an email), while other students from different cultures will opt for a very formal tone. The range of expectations from the instructor's side might also vary, based on their personal and ethnic background, micro culture, generation, and personal style.

Some instructors value a personable, casual, or even informal teaching style showing their occasional vulnerability, while others prefer establishing a certain classroom decorum. Whatever the approach selected, it is only fair to communicate one's expectations with students. A proactive approach is always a good idea, which may take the form of including a paragraph in that regard in the syllabus, for instance in a section titled "Communications with Instructor and Netiquette." In the same token, it is important to highlight the type of student-to-student interactions that are expected, and the behaviors that will not be tolerated. This is especially important for student discussions and any online socializing space (using Google Hangouts, VoiceThread, or any similar tool) created to replicate socializing spaces on campus. These spaces need to be clearly introduced to students as "non-monitored socializing spaces," as opposed to areas that are monitored by the instructors, for personal questions that might benefit the whole group, for instance.

Another important aspect of online education pertains to the frequency of communications to students (not *with* students). When the pandemic started, millions of teachers found themselves having to substitute face-to-face teaching with online teaching overnight. One of the authors saw firsthand how some high school teachers started inundating students with a massive number of notifications, leading to teenage students having to manage unreasonable numbers of daily notifications even after teachers had been teaching online for over a year. Sending information to higher education students who frequently choose asynchronous learning because of multiple (work and/or family) commitments outside their course of study need to be carefully considered. As mentioned at the beginning of this chapter, adequate planning and design of the syllabus and other content are key for lowering the need for and frequency of these notifications. While the frequency of announcements sent to the class reflects the instructor's individual teaching style, and while periodic announcements and class emails are reasonable to expect in any online course, daily announcements or emails are probably the result of poor planning or design. Finding the right amount of communication and its frequency is akin to an art, but instructors need to carefully consider that aspect of online teaching.

References

Anderson, T., L. Rourke, D.R. Garrison, W. Archer. Assessing teaching presence in a computer conference environment. *Journal of Asynchronous Learning Networks*, vol. 5, no. 2, 2001, pp. 1–17.

Costa, Karen. *99 Tips for Creating Simple and Sustainable Educational Videos: A Guide for Online Teachers and Flipped Classes.* Stylus Publishing, 2020.

Costa, Vonessa. *Healthcare Interpreting: Positioning to Thrive during a Pandemic.* University of Massachusetts Amherst, 2000, www.youtube.com/watch?v=3HL14JXa9K8&feature=youtu.be.

Farros, Jesslyn Nicole, et al. "Online Learning: The Effect of Synchronous Discussion Sessions in Asynchronous Courses." *Journal of Behavioral Education*, 2020.

Fowler, Rachel C. *The Effects of Synchronous Online Course Orientation on Student Attrition.* University of South Carolina, 2019, https://scholarcommons.sc.edu/etd/5346.

Garrison, D.R. "Communities of Inquiry in Online Learning: Social, Teaching and Cognitive Presence." *Encyclopedia of Distance and Online Learning*, 2009, pp. 352–5.
Garrison, D.R., et al. "Critical Thinking, Cognitive Presence, and Computer Conferencing in Distance Education'." *American Journal of Distance Learning*, vol. 15, no. 1, 2001.
Garrison, D.R., Terry Anderson, and Walter Archer. "Critical Inquiry in a Text-Based Environment: Computer Conferencing in Higher Education." *The Internet and Higher Education*, vol. 2, no. 2–3, 1999, pp. 87–105, https://doi.org/10.1016/S1096-7516(00)00016-6.
Heinberg, R. "Lightning Bolts and Illuminations." *Inner Knowing: Consciousness, Creativity, Insight and Intuition*, edited by H. Palmer. J. P. Tarcher/Putnam, 1998, pp. 124–30.
Jay-Rayon, Laurence Ibrahim Aibo, Elena Langdon, and Cristiano Mazzei. "Three Pedagogical Tools to Take Your Online Translation and Interpreting Course to the Next Level." *The ATA Chronicle*, Feb. 2020, www.ata-chronicle.online/featured/three-pedagogical-tools-to-take-your-online-translation-and-interpreting-courses-to-the-next-level/.
Martin, Florence, et al. "Bichronous Online Learning: Blending Asynchronous and Synchronous Online Learning." *Educause Review*, 8 Sept. 2020, https://er.educause.edu/articles/2020/9/bichronous-online-learning-blending-asynchronous-and-synchronous-online-learning.
Mazzei, Cristiano. "Subtitling Box Festival." 2020, https://youtu.be/VdmrI6JuEIM.
McGreal, Rory. *Online Education Using Learning Objects*. London: Routledge/Falmer, 2004. Print.
Rendón, Laura. *Sentipensante (Sensing, Thinking)*. Stylus Publishing, 2008.
Rendón, Laura. "Validating Culturally Diverse Students: Toward a New Model of Learning and Student Development." *Innovative Higher Education*, vol. 10, no. 1, 1994, pp. 33–50.
"Video Length in Online Classes: What Research Says." *Emporia State University*, 7 Apr. 2018, https://emporiastate.blogspot.com/2018/04/video-length-in-online-courses-what.html.
Washbourne, Kelly. "Beyond Error Marking: Written Corrective Feedback for a Dialogic Pedagogy in Translator Training." *The Interpreter and Translator Trainer*, vol. 8, no. 2, 2014, pp. 240–56.
"What Is the Digital Divide?" *The San Diego Foundation*, 19 Sept. 2020, www.sdfoundation.org/news-events/sdf-news/what-is-the-digital-divide/.
Yamagata-Lynch, Lisa C. "Blending Online Asynchronous and Synchronous Learning." *International Review of Research in Open and Distributed Learning*, vol. 15, no. 2, 2014, pp. 189–212.

5 Assessments, Rubrics, and Assignments

This chapter defines and conceptualizes assessments and rubrics, and provides examples of assignments used in various online synchronous and asynchronous translation and interpreting courses and workshops. While these assignments are framed for multilingual courses, they can be adapted to language-specific translation and interpreting courses.

5.1 Theory in Translator and Interpreter Training

Before discussing assessments, rubrics, and assignments, the authors would like to position themselves regarding the role of theory in translation and interpreting education. In the historical and still ongoing debate between those who claim that translator and interpreter training should focus exclusively on practice and those who argue for the inclusion of theory(ies) in teaching the next generation of professionals, the authors of this book favor the latter for a seemingly obvious reason. If one truly believes that the activities of translation and interpreting affect the lives of source and target audiences and practitioners with real consequences, be they positive or negative, one must agree that critical thinking about the activities as cultural phenomena and the actors participating in their dissemination should be one of the skills students develop in any educational experience. One way of fostering critical engagement with the tasks and their impact is to expose students to key texts in the field of translation and interpreting and their interdisciplinary connections, empirical research, and case studies about cross-cultural meaning negotiation, and encourage students to reflect on what they have read, watched, or listened to (in the case of video or podcast materials).

Unless instructors are teaching courses on translation or interpreting theories, in which students will be exposed to different trends in both disciplines—linguistic, sociolinguistic, philosophical, literary, cognitive, cultural studies, sociological, postcolonial, feminist, queer, race, etc.—the approaches the authors refer to are more aligned with what Andrew Chesterman discussed in a conversation with Emma Wagner in *Can Theory Help Translators? A Dialogue Between the Ivory Tower and the Wordface*. At one point, Chesterman, while trying to convince Wagner—who worked as

DOI: 10.4324/9781003149316-6

a translator, translation manager, and in other capacities for the European Commission for 30 years—about the importance and value of theory in professional translator and interpreter training, explains how the discipline has tried to move away from prescriptive approaches to more research-based ones that observe what translators actually do (2014, 3). He adds:

> [o]ne of the best contributions translation scholars can make to the work of professional translators is to study and then demonstrate the links between different translation decisions or strategies and the effects that such decisions or strategies seem to have on clients, readers, and cultures, both in the past and in the present, under given conditions. Such corroborated correlations between cause and effect should be part of a professional's awareness.
>
> (5–6)

It should thus be clear that the selection of texts to be discussed by students in courses geared toward professional development should inspire them to explore translation and interpreting beyond the reductive and simplistic lens of linguistic activities, to include conversations that view translators and interpreters as social actors and human beings participating in cultural exchanges, negotiating meaning that has consequences—some of them everlasting—for all those involved in the interactions. Not to mention that such exploration is also beneficial for students as future professional translators and interpreters in the sense that they, in turn, will be able to have more educated conversations with clients and commissioners about the demands of their work and their implications for target audiences.

5.2 Assessment

Creating effective learning assessments is a critical component of any instructional activity, and this is particularly complex in virtual classes. Instructors design assessment interactions with the goal of getting students to demonstrate the knowledge and skills defined in the learning outcomes of their courses. When adequately designed, assessments also engage and motivate students in the learning process and help instructors establish relationships with their students and among themselves if peer-to-peer feedback or group projects are also incorporated. Measuring students' progress also provides instructors with a clear idea of how students are doing in their classes and adjustments that need to be made to instruction or course content in case the majority of the students are performing poorly.

Assessment should be an ongoing practice in online courses and should include diagnostic (pre-assessment), formative, and summative examples (Anderson et al. 2001). Diagnostic tests are usually designed to test a learner's knowledge prior to learning. One way of doing that is to include a quiz or a survey in one's LMS to gauge students' pre-knowledge, interests, and expectations about course content. This will also help students become familiarized with the course's online environment while introducing them to an overview of what they are going to be exposed to in class. Such type of assessment can also be repeated at the end of the course so that instructors can have a better picture about what students have learned. In general, this type of diagnostic is not graded, since students are not expected to know anything about the topics being surveyed. However, based on the authors' online teaching experience, chances are student participation will increase exponentially if they receive some form of gratification for having participated in such diagnostic assessment in the form of a grade or extra points. Regardless, if graded, the weight of such evaluations should be lighter (low-stake assignment) compared to other forms of measuring students' progress in the course.

Formative assessments are conducted during the learning process, aimed at giving feedback to students about their work in progress and assisting them in correcting misunderstandings and missteps. Those include knowledge quizzes, low-stake translation and interpreting exercises, etc. For example, if one is introducing translation strategies via a pre-recorded PowerPoint lecture, a true or false or multiple-choice quiz at the end, or during the recording through polling (something that can be achieved with some smart video platforms geared toward higher education, such as Echo360[1]), will allow instructors to assess if students are able to recall important concepts. Summative assessments, on the other hand, require students to demonstrate their mastery level. Examples include term papers, high-stakes interpreting tests (such as synchronous final exams), translation projects, etc. There is a wealth of good information available online about effective assessments that instructors can easily access. All they need to do is use their favorite search engine and type in keywords such as "Center for Teaching and Learning" and "formative and summative assessment."

5.3 Learning Objectives and Outcomes

When thinking about different ways to measure students' knowledge and skills, instructors should make sure the types of assessments are aligned with their learning outcomes or objectives. Bloom's taxonomy, created in 1956, and reviewed and updated by several education scholars over the years (Anderson et al. 2001), still provides a good framework for different levels of learning, which, as mentioned, should be calibrated with what instructors want their students to learn and develop during their educational experience. Such objectives can be low level, as seen at the bottom of the following list (Figure 5.1), and can involve recalling information. One type of assessment that correlates with "remembering" would be short answer questions or a multiple-choice quiz, for instance. If the learning outcome is high level, students are then expected to create original work through assessment types such as a subtitling or a large translation project, interpreting exams, etc.

88 *Assessments, Rubrics, and Assignments*

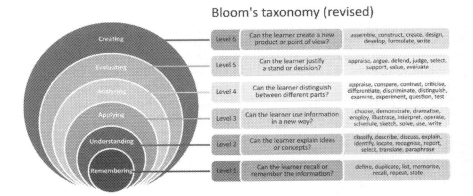

Figure 5.1 Bloom's Digital Taxonomy
Source: Used with permission—McNaulty

Again, going up and down the scale will depend heavily on what skills instructors want their students to learn or develop in class and how they are being asked to demonstrate that. Bloom's Digital Taxonomy (see Figure 5.1), revised by Andrew Churches in 2008 to help educators use technology and digital tools to facilitate learning (publicly available online), provides different types of assessments for each level of outcome that can be used in the online environment. For example, for the learning objective of "applying," Churches offer suggestions such as students demonstrating they have learned a concept by making a presentation with the use of recorded PowerPoint or creating a podcast from an interview (2008, 21).

The following is an example of learning objectives for an online CAT Tools for Translators course currently offered by the University of Massachusetts Amherst:

"Learning Outcomes
At the end of this course, students should be able to:

- Discuss theoretical issues related to automated translation programs
- Carry out advanced Internet searches
- Build personal concept-oriented Term Bases
- Interact with CAT tools
- Create and identify coded translatable text using HTML for translators"

When designing different types of assessments, instructors should be constantly going back to their course objectives and should inquire about their alignment with assessment tools. If we use these learning outcomes as an example, such questions include, "How am I going to *measure* if the student is able to discuss theoretical issues related to automated translation programs?" A straightforward answer and type of assessment selected could be discussion forums or short reaction papers.

5.4 Rubrics

Rubrics are scoring devices used by instructors to provide feedback, mark their students' class assignments and homework, and lay out specific instructor expectations regarding students' performance. Such tools also include detailed descriptions of acceptable and unacceptable levels of performance and a breakdown of the assignment into smaller parts. However, rubrics are also extremely useful devices that students can use for self-assessment and reflections, as discussed in Chapter 2. According to Stevens & Levi, they allow students to "notice for themselves the patterns of recurring problems or ongoing improvement in their work, and this self-discovery is one of the happiest outcomes of using rubrics" (2012, 33). Such tools also encourage students to think critically about their own learning and motivate them to continue practicing and learning.

Rubrics can be designed by instructors or be co-constructed by students, fostering accountability in their learning process and creating a collaborative environment. In "Interpreting Quality as Perceived by Trainee Interpreters," Magdalena Bartlomiejczyk talks about the importance of moving away from the traditional "error analysis" model used in assessing interpreting performance, arguing that it "does not recognize differences in standards applied to conference interpreting and written translation" (2007, 248). She goes on to discuss the importance of assigning different weights to different aspects of performance. The same argument is echoed by Jung Yoon Choi in "Metacognitive Evaluation Method in Consecutive Interpretation for Novice Learners," in which she posits that the evaluation methods for novice interpreters should be different from those used to measure the performance of professional interpreters (2006, 273). Choi also shares that "students are overconcerned with even the slightest errors, thus sometimes negatively affecting the entire performance" (274). For example, it might be a good idea to assign less weight to minor inappropriate interpretation solutions for beginning students, such as grammar, register, regionalisms, and delivery (hesitations, hedging, etc.), and heavier weight to meaning, which is what students are taught to focus on as they practice consecutive interpretation exercises. Obviously, as they progress to more complex interpreting assignments toward mastery, weights will change.

When teaching glossary development, educators in general want students to develop a deeper understanding of the concept of confirming the best target translation solution for source-language terms in reputable sources—be they online dictionaries, parallel texts, or encyclopedias. Thus, it seems reasonable to assign heavier weight to the "references" and the "target translation" columns, and lighter weights to elements such as "source term/linguistic category (noun, adj., verb, etc.)" and "definition/context" (see Table 5.1).

Table 5.1 Glossary Rubric

Source	Definition	Context	Target Translation	Reference
Please include here the original English word or phrase. Indicate the part of speech it belongs to (noun, verb, adjective, etc.). Make sure that the translation in the "Target Translation" column corresponds to the same part of speech as the original. For instance, if the term in the source is a "verb," your translation must also be a "verb" (noun, adjective, adverb, etc.).	Include here a definition from a reliable source (monolingual dictionary, encyclopedia, etc.). Indicate where you found the definition. Do not include a definition of what YOU THINK the word or phrase means.	Words and phrases without context are often meaningless. It is very important that you include here the sentence in which the word/phrase appears. For instance, if your technical word/phrase is "filling" as in dentistry, include the sentence where it appeared. For instance, "Your fillings can easily break from eating foods that are too hard or chewy."	Include here the target translation. Make sure it corresponds to the same part of speech as the source (noun, verb, adjective, etc.)!	**Very important!** Please include here where you found the target translation (names of dictionaries, URLs from the Internet, parallel texts, articles, expert opinions, etc.)

Elements	Weight
1 <u>Source</u>: Includes the English term (word or phrase) appropriately. Makes sure it is a specialized term and not a common term (if it's easily found in a regular bilingual dictionary, it should not be in a specialized glossary). No spelling mistakes. Indicates the part of speech it belongs to in the context (noun, verb, adjective, etc.).	5
2 <u>Definition</u>: Includes a definition from a reliable source and indicates it: dictionaries (online or offline), encyclopedias (online or offline).	10
3 <u>Context</u>: Includes the sentence where the term (word or phrase) was found in the source.	10
4 <u>Target translation</u>: Includes the target translation, following all the appropriate linguistic rules of the language (includes accent markers, etc.). Make sure it belongs to the same part of speech as the source (noun, verb, adjective, etc.).	20
5 <u>Reference</u>: Includes reference regarding where the target translation was found being used in context (dictionaries [online/offline], websites, parallel texts, articles, etc.).	15
TOTAL	60

Criteria	Outstanding	Good	Fair	Incomplete
1 Source	5	4	3	2
2 Definition	10	8	7	3
3 Context	10	8	7	3
4 Target Translation	20	18	17	12
5 Reference	15	12	11	10
TOTAL	60	50	45	30

5.5 Assignments

As discussed in Chapter 2, since translation and interpreting are skills that need to be practiced over time to be performed at professional levels, educational initiatives should offer engaging activities and authentic materials. The term "assignment" is being used here to refer generally to learning experiences students engage with in different online classes and workshops. Without being exhaustive, the following list suggests a few categories of assignments:

1. theoretical discussions
2. translation of texts
3. interpretation of pre-recorded audio or video files
4. subtitling exercises
5. live/synchronous interpreting exams

In the following examples provided, which are used across a variety of translation and interpretation courses, we will first describe the assignment, then explain how it can be assessed by instructors, students, or their peers, and last discuss the rubric that can be used for evaluation by educators or self-assessment by students.

5.5.1 Theoretical Discussions

Let us look at some examples that could be used for online discussion and critical skill building based on what was described previously. If one is teaching a class or a module on simultaneous interpreting, students might benefit from reading (listening or watching) and discussing texts focused on cognitive constraints of the task or empirical research of interpreters during practice (Seleskovitch 2001; Lederer 1978; Chernov 1994; Altman 1994; Gile 2009). Such conversations can take place in traditional discussion forums or more contemporary variations, such as VoiceThread (see full discussion of the tool in Chapter 3).

Discussion Forum

As a spin-off from electronic mailing lists, listservs, or web-based bulletin boards, with the goal of creating virtual communities of regular users exchanging ideas, asynchronous discussion forums have been a staple in distance learning for decades, providing a platform through which instructors and students can engage with topics at deeper levels, according to Bloom's Taxonomy (see previous discussion). In a recent article in *The Chronicle of Higher Education*, Mark Lieberman surveys several instructional designers and their opinions about the value of discussion forums in online courses, by stating in the beginning of his piece, "instructors and students alike are growing tired of the discussion board formula" (2019, n. pag.). Historically, this engagement tool has been utilized as an assignment for students to respond to assigned readings, videos, podcasts, etc., and engage with the topic while collaborating with their peers in acquiring knowledge and deeper understanding of topics, something very similar to lively discussions that take place in in-person classrooms. However, in search of different strategies to revamp the decades-old virtual community space, instructors are coming up with different ways to approach it. One of them "is to emphasize quality and thoughtfulness of responses over quantity and frequency," (Lieberman). Others include establishing deadlines for students to submit their initial post and allowing students to add entries in the forum by using different types of media instead of a written text (PowerPoint presentations with audio, mind maps, audios, videos, etc.). No matter how instructors set up their discussion forum, most students will only participate if they are receiving credit for it. While motivated students will likely contribute to the conversations without the extra points, instructors will also want to assess all their students' deeper learning resulting from discussion forums, hence grading them seems the right way to go.

One rubric used by the authors of this book echoes Lieberman's comments about quality over quantity and encourages students to interact with each other to foster a sense of community (see Table 5.2). Moreover, one way to stimulate accountability in students regarding their own learning is to select different students to be "discussion leaders," which can be done in the first week of class by asking students to select one or two articles (or videos, podcasts, etc.) to kick off the discussion forums. This can be easily done by sharing a Google Doc with students and giving them a deadline to sign up for selected texts or by placing the bibliography list inside the LMS. Instructors can also model it and guide the discussion by posting one or two questions about the topic.

Table 5.2 Online Discussion Rubric

IMPORTANT: In order to get the full grade for each discussion online, you need to **post/answer** one comment/question regarding the article, video, podcast, etc., and **comment on** two posts from other classmates, according to the criteria in the rubric.

Posts		Comments/Dialogue	
Quantity: Discusses major takeaways and points in sufficient length and depth (min 100—max 150 words).	Quality: Supports opinions with examples and evidence; includes specifics rather than generalities.	Quantity: Responds to at least two POSTS from other students for each discussion topic (min 50—max 100 words).	Quality: Moves beyond "good point" and "I agree," to raise new points, expand the topic, and ask questions.

94 *Assessments, Rubrics, and Assignments*

There is abundant information available online about discussion forums and how to assess and create questions for them, including "Writing Discussion Forum Questions" (McDonald 2016). The same activity can be performed with new technologies such as VoiceThread, which allows students to post questions and comments using text, audio, video, or another type of media (see Chapter 3). This scoring device can be further enhanced by adding exemplars of excellent, good, fair, and incomplete types of engagement in the discussion space, as illustrated in the following example of a discussion on professional codes of ethics and standards from different organizations:

"**Prompt**: Codes of ethics and standards of practice guide the conduct of translators and interpreters. Many authors, including Mason and Ren, have stated that the traditional view of T&Is as mere conduits, invisible and powerless in the exchange, is an illusion. Such a view, however, is encouraged by some professional organizations in their codes of ethics. According to these authors, a non-traditional view where T&Is are co-participants, portrays a more realistic perspective. When reviewing the three codes of ethics

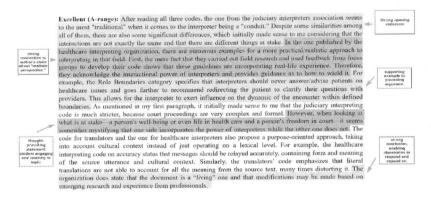

Figure 5.2 Exemplar of "Excellent" Engagement

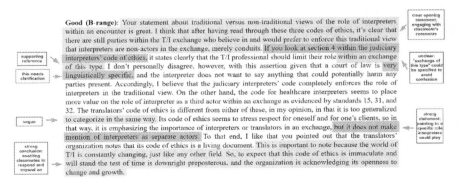

Figure 5.3 Exemplar of "Good" Engagement

Assessments, Rubrics, and Assignments 95

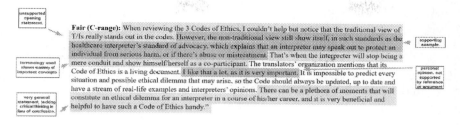

Figure 5.4 Exemplar of "Fair" Engagement

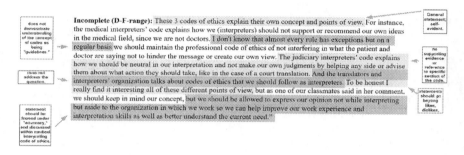

Figure 5.5 Exemplar of "Incomplete" Engagement

referenced in the exercise, what are some examples of standards of practice that illustrate how traditional views are perpetuated?"

"Please review the exemplars in Figures 5.2, 5.3, 5.4, and 5.5 for expectations regarding your engagement with the prompt and your classmates' comments."

5.5.2 Translation of Texts

In multilingual online translation courses, the issue of directionality is a very interesting one. Ideally, students should be screened before starting their classes to check for similar proficiency levels in their language pair. Considering that they are at similar levels, it should not really matter in which direction they are going into. The authors of this book recognize that there is an ongoing, decades-old heated debate about the issue, with the prevailing notion in some powerful Western countries that one should only translate into one's "mother tongue," which seems to be rooted in a "Romantic identification of the transcendental nature of the nation and its language," with the main argument being that the "essence" of the target language cannot be accessed by any "foreign speaker" (Pokorn 2000, 61). In a blog post, Floriana Badalotti reminds us of the interesting paradox that lies within such assumption,

> if we assume that a native speaker of the target language is better equipped to translate the nuances of meaning of the source text, shouldn't a native speaker of the source language be better equipped to understand these nuances in the first place?
>
> (2019)

Without wishing to offend anyone, our view is that supply and demand in different geographic locations and contexts should really dictate directionality. Working bidirectionally is a common practice in places such as Brazil, Australia, and the Netherlands, for example, not to mention many other countries around the world. One of the authors of this book has spent most of his professional translator life successfully working into his second language, or L2, as opposed to his native one, or L1.

In multilingual societies around the world, where residents of the same country speak multiple languages, directionality does not seem to be an issue, something that should be reflected in curricula. Lamenting the current English-French focused landscape of translation and interpreting training in the Democratic Republic of Congo, Emmanuel Kambaja Musampa calls for the inclusion of Congolese languages in the curriculum (160 to 260 languages from different linguistic families), stating that such national languages are sadly being viewed as ""barrières" à différents niveaux et dans différents contextes de communication" (as "hurdles" in many regards and in different communication settings) (2021, 102). According to Kuto, the official languages of many African countries are still those of their former colonizers (English, French, Portuguese, and Spanish), with citizens who do not speak them being excluded from participation in society, constantly finding themselves translating in and out of their indigenous languages, and creating a "universal directionality, that is, translation from and into all languages of the jurisdiction" (2021, 116). Moreover, "communities which use 'a language of restricted distribution or limited diffusion,'" are "forced to translate into foreign languages if they want their works to be translated at all," adds Pokorn (68). An interesting experiment conducted by Tony Parr, a professional business translator, to test the "mother tongue principle," revealed unexpected results. Bar and a colleague asked six Dutch-speaking translation commissioners and six English-speaking language professionals to decide which was the best English translation (out of a group of four) of a 300-word Dutch passage from a museum brochure. Two of them were translated by native speakers of Dutch, and two by professionals whose native language was English—all experienced translators. Interestingly, the English panel thought the best translation was the one performed by the native Dutch-speaking translator, who translated the passage into their L2 (Parr 2016).

Whatever principle they want to follow, one thing all instructors will agree on is that textual translation should be one of the main components in a translator training course or module, in addition to subcompetences such as terminology search, subject matter research, etc. The following is a simple translation exercise, followed by a process-oriented assessment method and rubric. As mentioned elsewhere, instructions for exercises in online courses must be as clear as possible and, if possible, presented in different ways and places inside the LMS.

"**Translation Exercise Instructions**

Students are encouraged[2] to translate this short text (recipe/cooking) from English into their LOTE, and submit the first draft to the appropriate box (the file should be named and saved with the student's name—for instance, as "**cooking_mazzei_draft**"). Please apply all the knowledge you have acquired in the first weeks of the course in your process, including thinking about different strategies, target audience, term search, etc., while translating the text. Your first draft should be accompanied by a short reflection on the strategies you used to resolve ONE specific issue (a word, a term, a phrase), and resources used. For an example of reflection, see the document titled "**Translation_Reflection_Model**" in your course shell. Students will receive feedback from the instructor on their reflections and then have one more week to use such input and work on their final draft, which should be submitted to the appropriate box by the posted deadline (the file should be named and saved with the student's name, as in "**cooking_mazzei_final**"). Students are encouraged to not use Google Translate or any other automatic translation software or website."

This exercise presents the assignment as a two-phase process, which works really well for both language-specific and multilingual classes. Students will initially translate and reflect on their performance, receive feedback from their instructor on their reflections, and then use the input to go back to the same text to work on a final version. The final translation is then sent to an external language reviewer if the student is enrolled in a language-neutral course or assessed by instructors themselves in language-specific courses.

As can be noticed in this example rubric, and rooted in UDL as discussed in Chapter 1, the rubric is composed of guiding questions that students can use as they write observations about their own work (or record an audio, video, etc.). Moreover, a reflection template is also made available to make the instructor's expectations about the students' deep-level engagement with the task absolutely clear.

5.5.3 *Interpretation of Pre-Recorded Audio or Video Files*

One of the main aims of teaching consecutive interpretation, or any other interpreting mode, is for students to develop interpreting skills. While the importance of critical thinking, and how to explore and apply it as educational practice, was briefly discussed previously, we will now discuss interpreting performance as such. Most instructors will follow scaffolding approaches, in which less complicated speeches are used first, with students moving to more complex audio and video files during the course. No matter how educators structure their classes, speeches and different types of "talk" should be authentic representations of settings and subject matter students will encounter in their professional lives. There are several resources available online, in addition to textbooks with accompanying audio and video materials, but most of them have been developed for a specific area of the field, which is conference interpreting. If one is teaching community translation and interpreting, resources are scarcer, and instructors have to spend a lot of time digging for them online. One recommendation is to search for community organizations that provide services to immigrant populations in different countries around the world, and government agencies which produce translated content for new immigrants, including video that can be used for interpreting exercises. However, more often than not, instructors will spend a lot of time developing and collecting their own materials, for example, creating role-plays, selecting specific source texts to be used in T&I activities to meet the specific needs of their learning objectives, especially in multilingual courses. Students are also encouraged to produce materials in different languages that can be shared and practiced on by their classmates. After being exposed to different exercises to develop their analytical, memory, and note-taking skills, students should be ready to perform consecutive interpretation. The following is an example of an interpreting assignment description.

Interpreting Exercise Instructions—Long Consecutive with Notes
"The topic/subject of the audio you're about to listen to is 'baby nutrition.' **Prepare and Practice:** Please review information online (different websites, watch videos about the topic, etc.) about the topic since, as you know by now, the more knowledgeable you are about a subject the better you'll be able to understand, analyze it, and render your interpretation. I have added some materials under the "practice folder" that you can also use. Prepare symbols and abbreviations for different concepts related to the topic and practice note-taking. Under the **VoiceThread** (discussed in Chapter 3) "Long Consecutive Safe Practice Space," students are encouraged to record and submit original speeches on the topic so that their classmates can practice on.

Assignment: For this assignment, you'll need to play an audio file, use a notepad (according to instructions) to take notes, and use a device to record your interpretation. When ready, play and listen to the audio "**baby nutrition.mp3**" only once. Do not listen to it beforehand. Take notes while listening to the audio file. Then, press your recording device (you can use your smartphone) and perform interpretation into your target language from your memory and notes. Submit your audio file, image (pic) of your notes, and a short reflection based on the rubric provided (text, audio, or video). You should submit at least three different files. Please refer to the

"Interpreting Reflection Template" to learn about the expectations for your self-assessment."

As one can see from the instructions in this example, a "safe space" has been created inside a rich media interactive tool (VoiceThread) for students to share original speeches and practice their long consecutive interpretation. This approach entails many benefits, including students practicing their "public speaking" skills, note-taking, and interpreting in a collaborative environment. They can also be encouraged to give each other feedback, etc. In multilingual environments, students can also give each other feedback in terms of sound quality, tone of voice, hesitations, etc.

For both reflective practice rubrics (see Tables 5.3 and 5.4), instructors can decide to break down the activity into parts and grade them according to their objectives. Table 5.5 shows an example that educators can adapt as needed (and further modify to a translation or interpreting assignment). Let us imagine that the reflection is worth ten points in a total of ten reflections students will perform during the course, which corresponds to 20% of their overall grade.

Table 5.3 Translation Process Reflection Rubric

As you work on your translation and think about the process, please include some of the following in your reflection as appropriate:

Translation Process:
- How did you find the target translation for the most difficult word/term/phrase?
- How do you know your translation of the most difficult word/term/phrase is correct?
- Did you think about the audience as you were translating?

Translation tools and resources:
- Which tools did you use to help you in your translations (dictionaries, glossaries, online searches)? Please be specific and name your sources.
- Did you ask someone/an expert for help? Please be specific.
- Did you post a question to a translators' forum or group on Facebook or other listservs?

Translation Unit/Challenge:
- Which word or term was the most difficult word/term/phrase (took you the longest) to translate? Why? Is it technical? Be specific and please provide a back/gloss translation into English if focusing on a LOTE term.
- Is the word/term/phrase culturally specific?

Translation Strategies:
- Which strategy did you use to solve a translation unit/challenge? Reformulation? Explicitation? Paraphrasing? Reduction? Footnote? Cultural Substitution? Etc.

Translation Quality:
- Did you proofread your target text after you finished?
- Did you use Spell Check in Word or another spelling tool?

Time spent on translation:
- How long did it take you to translate this text?
- Do you feel your linguistic skills in the source and target languages played a role in how long it took?

Continue

As you work on your translation and think about the process, please include some of the following in your reflection as appropriate:

Translation Discovery:
- What new thing did you learn while you were working on this translation?
- How did you feel when you were done?
- Were you satisfied with the result?

Improvement Plans:
- Do you need to take more high-level classes in your LOTE or English to improve your linguistic performance?
- Do you need to take high-level writing courses?
- Should you improve your general knowledge? Specialized knowledge?

A prior version of this rubric has been published in the article "Three Pedagogical Tools to Take your Online Translation and Interpreting Course to the Next Level" [Jay-Rayon, Langdon, and Mazzei 2020].

Table 5.4 Rubric for Interpreting Reflection

As you listen to your interpretation, use some of the questions in this rubric to reflect on your performance:

Delivery:
- How does your voice sound? Can you hear yourself clearly? Hesitant? Confident? If hesitant, why?
- Did you overcorrect yourself (back tracking)?
- How was your pronunciation?

Meaning:
- Did you not come up with the best possible translation in the target language? (Be specific when reflecting).
- Did you come across a term/word/phrase/expression you didn't know? What was the solution?
- Did you guess the target translation and it turned out to be the appropriate one when you searched parallel texts?
- Which strategy did you use to solve the interpreting challenge? Reformulation? Explanation? Borrowing? Calque? (Be specific about this example—provide a back/gloss translation into English if working into LOTE.

Omissions:
- Did you decide not to provide a translation for an acronym/abbreviation? Explain.
- Did you omit something you didn't know the translation for? Why? What different strategy could you have used?
- Did you omit something that did not impact/change the meaning of the speech segment?

Notes:
- Did you prepare and practice your notes before the exercise? Did you come up with good symbols and abbreviations?
- Did the notes interfere with your interpretation? How?
- Did taking notes interfere with your listening and understanding of the speech?

Interpreting Discovery:
- What new thing did you learn about your interpreting skills?
- How did you feel during your performance? After?
- How do you feel about the result of your performance? (Provide examples of successful interpreting strategies.)

As you listen to your interpretation, use some of the questions in this rubric to reflect on your performance:

Improvement Plans:
- After identifying the issue(s), what is your plan for improvement?
- Should you work more on analysis and memory skills?
- Do you need to take more high-level classes in your LOTE or English to improve your linguistic performance?
- Should you increase the number of times you practice every week? Day?
- Should you find ways to feel more relaxed when interpreting? Mindfulness exercises?

Table 5.5 Weighted Rubric for T&I Process Reflections

Elements	Weight
1 Translation challenge(s): Describe at least one example of translation challenge and discuss how you addressed it.	5
2 Successful strategy: Describe at least one example of a successful performance (reformulation, using the best target translation, cultural substitution, etc.) and provide evidence to confirm the target challenge is used in context.	3
3 Plans for improvement: Based on issues identified, describe how you plan to address them with specific details.	2
TOTAL	10

Criteria	Outstanding	Good	Fair	Incomplete
1 Translation challenge	5	4.7	4	3
2 Successful strategy	3	2.6	2.3	1.7
3 Plans for improvement	2	1.4	1	0.8
TOTAL	10	8.7	7.3	5.5

5.5.4 Subtitling Exercises

The following is an example of a subtitling assignment description in an audiovisual translation course. One of the expectations, which can even become a learning outcome, in audiovisual translation or subtitling courses, is for students to become independent problem-solvers. Technology evolves at such a pace that subtitlers have to constantly adapt to a variety of subtitling platforms and tools, and file formats. It is important to communicate this expectation at the beginning of the course, for instance in the form of a paragraph in the syllabus. This will alleviate frustration from those students who are used to instructors holding their hand every step of the way.

"Subtitling Activity Description

Before you begin your translation into your LOTE and add subtitles, make sure you review the subtitling standards introduced and explored so far and the subtitling rubric provided for this assignment. Your subtitled video will be sent to language-specific reviewers.

SUBTITLING TOOL OPTIONS

1 You can use the free subtitle software Subtitle Workshop. See the instruction manual to get started. Additionally, there are many video tutorials and discussions available online regarding Subtitle Workshop. You will need to convert the mp4 video file into an. avi video file to get the best results with Subtitle Workshop.
2 You can use the free subtitle software Aegisub. **For macOS users,** you can download it here: www.macupdate.com/app/mac/33388/aegisub. One of your classmates tried it and informed me of the following: 'Apple has a security feature where it won't let you open apps it can't verify (meaning that they weren't downloaded from the App Store or from a trusted developer). To be able to open Aegisub for the first time, you have to go to Finder, right click Aegisub, and click Open, only then will it give you the option to actually open it. After opening it like this for the first time, the next time you want to open it, it will now allow you to do so by double-clicking like any normal app would.' **For Windows users,** you can download it here: www.filehorse.com/download-aegisub-64/
See Aegisub Video Tutorials listed here:

   1 Getting Started video (about 7 minutes): www.youtube.com/watch?v=4gXF6Y-v6BE
   2 Moving and resizing text: www.youtube.com/watch?v=gopfzv6tZYA
   3 Editing font, color, and customizing: www.youtube.com/watch?v=ypqiBbtFCG8
   4 Exporting and saving subtitles: www.youtube.com/watch?v=AF69Y63yiWw
   5 Hardcoding (aka "burning" the subtitles onto the video): www.youtube.com/watch?v=QDwNn4NU1io

3 You can use the free trial version of the professional tool of your choice, based on the comparative analysis you did in Week 3 (OOONA, EZTitles, or Spot Software, to name but a few). You explored many of them in Week 3.

BURNING SUBTITLES ONTO THE VIDEO

After you are done creating your subtitles, there is still another step. You will need to hardcode (burn) the subtitles onto the video file.

VLC and Handbrake are the free tools suggested to do so (apparently Handbrake works better with macOS). You will find two tutorials, one for VLC, one for Handbrake, included in Week 5 Assignments folder to show you how to hardcode subtitles.

BEFORE SUBMITTING YOUR FILE (.mp4 file)

1. Make sure to NAME your file correctly (see Syllabus). This is very important as your file will be sent to language reviewers.
2. Make sure that your video plays well and that the subtitles show well on your end.
3. Try sending your hardcoded video file to a friend or family member. Ask them to watch it and tell you if the subtitles show well and are synchronized.
4. Submit your file to the assignment box as an. mp4 file."

The following rubric (see Table 5.6) is included in the assignment folder, along with the video file of the movie clip to translate and all the tutorials mentioned in the assignment description.

Language reviewers are asked to provide comments on the first two criteria, "adaptation and condensation" and "translation quality and language mechanics," while the instructor will focus on non-language-specific aspects described in the last two criteria "segmentation and synchronization" and "compliance with subtitling conventions," which can be adapted for non-Western languages.

5.5.5 *Live/Synchronous Interpreting Exams*

A few words of caution about live exams include informing students of the day of the exam ahead of time. It helps to include the date on the syllabus and remind students that such a date is non-negotiable, since it requires careful organization and planning from the instructor who will need to secure the availability of language reviewers to play the role of the LOTE speaker in the role-play, as specified in the assignment description that follows. It is challenging for some students to accept a live exam component in online courses. It is therefore a good idea to announce it early and repeat it at regular intervals during the course to avoid unnecessary difficulties. The second challenge is to make sure that all students are aware of their own time zone. Students taking online courses can be in time zones that are different from that of their instructors or the learning institution. It is therefore crucial to repeat, in different ways and forms, that the time slots on the live exam schedule are expressed in such or such a time zone. Mundane as it may be, this word of caution will go a long way to avoid frustration for the instructor and distress for students who will "have forgotten" to convert the time slot of their live exam into their own time zones. The following is a sample description of a live exam in a medical interpretation setting. Instructors will send the role-play script ahead of time to the language reviewers to give them time to translate their lines into their LOTE and prepare playing the role of the LOTE patient. On live video platforms such as Zoom, it is very easy to open another

Table 5.6 Subtitling Rubric

	Outstanding A range	Good B Range	Fair C range	Incomplete D to F range
Adaptation and condensation	Effectively re-expresses the meaning and all the nuances of the source text (ST) while managing to adequately condense the message. Consistently uses adequate target language equivalents, successfully producing high quality subtitles that convey the meaning of the feature film/video. Fully identifies translation/ adaptation challenges and makes effective decisions to solve them.	Re-expresses the meaning and some nuances of the ST while managing to adequately condense the message. Uses adequate target language equivalents, successfully producing quality subtitles that convey the meaning of the feature film/video. Generally, identifies translation/ adaptation challenges and makes effective decisions to solve them.	Re-expresses some the meaning of the ST and somehow manages to condense the message. Inconsistently uses target language equivalents. Partially identifies translation/ adaptation challenges, thus not generally making effective decisions to solve them.	Does not convey core elements of meaning. Difficulty condensing message. Fails to identify translation/ adaptation challenges to come up with effective decisions to solve them.
Translation quality and language mechanics	Language mechanics are excellent throughout. Appropriate interpretation of source text and reformulation in target language/ culture, thus making effective translation choices.	Good grasp of language mechanics. Minor issues in interpreting source text and reformulating in target language/ culture.	Some issues of literal or word-for-word translations, ST syntax interference (word order). Some issues in translation choices (interpreting source text/ reformulating in target language/ culture).	Numerous issues of literal or word-for-word translation. ST syntax interference (word order) numerous words misspelled, typos, etc. Major inappropriate translation choices.

Segmentation and synchronization	Segments all subtitles in a precise manner, taking into account enunciations in the scene/shot. Takes into consideration the 1- and 6-second principles. Synchronizes all subtitles with enunciations.	Segments most subtitles in a precise manner, taking into account enunciations in the scene/shot. For the most part, takes into consideration the 1- and 6-second principles. Synchronizes most subtitles with enunciations. Minor instances of delayed or too advanced appearance of subtitles, causing minor out-of-sync issues.	Segments some subtitles in a precise manner, taking into account enunciations in the scene/shot. Irregularly takes into consideration the 1- and 6-second principles. Synchronizes some subtitles with enunciations. Major instances of delayed or too advanced appearance of subtitles, causing major out-of-sync issues.	Demonstrates poor grasp of segmentation principles. Does not take into account enunciation in the scene/shot. Does not apply the 1- and 6-second principles. Unsuccessful synchronization.
Compliance with conventions	Fully complies with conventions and norms (typography, italics, position on screen, balanced two lines; avoids duplicating information conveyed visually or orally).	Mostly complies with conventions and norms (typography, italics, position on screen, balanced two lines; avoids duplicating information conveyed visually or orally).	Somehow complies with conventions and norms (typography, italics, position on screen, balanced two lines; avoids duplicating information conveyed visually or orally).	Does not comply with conventions and norms (typography, italics, position on screen, balanced two lines; avoids duplicating information conveyed visually or orally).

window and read the script directly from one's screen, so as to be facing the camera for video recording purposes. Each live exam is video-recorded and, for instructors using Zoom, we recommend using the cloud recording option, which is the easiest to share with others. The instructor will receive a shareable URL in their inbox, which can in turn be easily shared with language reviewers and students. Below is a sample of final exam instructions.

"**Medical Interpretation Course: Final Exam Description**
The following is the final exam schedule with your individual time slots. [Insert link to Google Doc sign-up sheet with available time slots. Include time zone.]
Consecutive Interpreting, Medical Dialogue
You will be taking your exam in the consecutive Video Remote Interpreting (VRI) mode on Zoom.

Come Equipped:

- Note pad and pens (second pen as a backup).
- Computer and headset.
- Ethernet connection if possible. Otherwise, strong wifi connection.
- Backup plan (Zoom downloaded and signed in on your **charged** phone or tablet in case your computer fails), **write down or print Zoom meeting ID and info**.
- Log into the Zoom meeting about 15 minutes prior to your time slot. You will be automatically placed in the waiting room. I will let you in when it is your turn.

Come Prepared:

- Prepare for topic: **Medical Visit/Domestic Violence.**
- Practice strategies to professionally manage the flow of conversation if you need repeats or clarifications.
- Practice consecutive interpreting with note-taking, like you did during the semester.

What to Expect:

- I will play the role of the English speaker.
- The language reviewer will play the role of the LOTE speaker.
- Each exam will be video recorded and used by language reviewers to review and evaluate your performance. You will also receive a copy of the video recording to help you review what went well and what you can work on.
- Use the attached interpretation performance rubric to help you prepare. Language reviewers will use the same rubric to write their feedback.

Zoom Meeting Information:
[Include appropriate login information with meeting number]"

As seen from Table 5.7, the remote dialogue interpreting rubric is broken down into two major performance criteria: translation/interpreting skills, and professional standards, which are further broken down into smaller categories, aligned with the course's learning objectives. Moreover, in online T&I courses, students must also incorporate best practices for remote dialogue interpreting via teleconferencing platforms, including being mindful of how their surroundings look if the camera is on, the quality of the audio and camera, Internet connection speed, and professional attire (see "Pre-Professional Practice Collaborations" in Chapter 6). In multilingual courses, language reviewers will focus mostly on language mechanics, while instructors, who are experts teaching T&I skills, standards, and ethics, are responsible for providing feedback on such criteria. The following is an excerpt of feedback from the reviewer and instructor for the same student working with the English/Spanish pair:

Reviewer
"Student used formal and informal tenses inconsistently (mostly use of *tú*, but sometimes used '*escuche*' or '*ha sentido este dolor antes*'—*usted* forms). Use of literal translation producing a non-existing word in Spanish, '*contracepciones.*' Although the term '*contracepción*' exists in Spanish, it should only be used in singular. Sometimes the student forgets they are the interpreter, and asks the patient as if they were the doctor, '*¿qué específicamente le duele?*'

The student conveys to doctor that the patient's boyfriend 'hit her,' which was never said by the patient. The patient also tells the doctor that her boyfriend is a good man, but the interpreter never translates that. When the doctor says to the patient that her boyfriend should not "hurt" her, she translated "*tu novio no debería darte,*" which changes the semantic field, implying hitting."

Instructor
"Introduction: Good introduction! However, you could have added other things in your introduction, such as information about confidentiality, direct communication, something about situational management, such as 'I might ask you to pause or ask for repetition or clarifications.'

Situational Management: In the first question from doctor to patient, you took control over the conversation by adding something the doctor never said. In this case, you made the decision to take on the role of the doctor, instead of allowing the doctor to make that decision for themselves. In addition to that, you were not transparent about this added conversation with the patient, and the doctor had no idea what was going on.

Clarifies Misunderstandings: You did a good job asking for repetition in the last part where the patient talks for a long time, when she says that she thinks "it's her fault." However, there are effective ways to ask for

108 *Assessments, Rubrics, and Assignments*

Table 5.7 Remote Dialogue Interpreting Rubric

Language	Excellent 100–90%	Good 80–70%	Fair 60–50%	Incomplete Below 50%
Translation/ interpreting skills	Shows evidence of mastery. Uses appropriate target language solutions. No use of literal translations that impede communication. Appropriate use of translation strategies, such as reformulations, cultural equivalents, etc. No omission of important information nor distortions of meaning.	Shows significant evidence of mastery. For the most part, uses appropriate translation solutions, including reformulations. Despite some use of inappropriate literal translation, it does not impede communication. There were some, but no serious omissions or distortions of meaning.	Shows fair evidence of mastery. However, there is frequent use of inappropriate literal translation, sometimes impeding communication. Infrequent use of appropriate translation strategies, frequent use of inappropriate borrowings that somewhat impede communication. Some omissions were inappropriate and caused partial understanding of message. Some distortions of meaning.	Shows limited evidence or no mastery of language conversion concepts, causing communication to break down. There were many omissions and distortions of meaning.
Language mechanics	Shows evidence of appropriate use of language (grammar and syntax).	Uses language appropriately, but there are a few issues of grammar and syntax.	Frequent issues of grammar and syntax.	Many issues of grammar and syntax.
Delivery/ production	Pronunciation, tone, and diction is excellent and does not impede understanding. Confident delivery, with almost no hesitations.	Pronunciation, tone, and diction are appropriate, but some minor deviations from idiomatic use are noticed. Comprehension maybe slightly compromised, but not often—maybe caused by nervousness.	Pronunciation, tone, and diction somewhat interfere with meaning. Comprehension is somewhat compromised by several issues.	Pronunciation, tone, and diction interfere with meaning to the point that communication breaks down.

	Excellent	Good	Fair	Incomplete
Specialized language and register	Correct use of technical/medical terms and use of appropriate language register.	Technical/medical terms were mostly correct. Language register was mostly adequate.	Displays inconsistent use of technical/medical terms (inappropriate use of borrowed terms, etc.), and use of inappropriate language register, somewhat impeding communication.	Does not translate technical/medical terms appropriately at all. Inappropriate use of language register.

TOTAL

	Excellent	Good	Fair	Incomplete
Standards of Practice/Ethics/Professionalism				
Proper introduction	Excellent performance. Includes important information in both languages, including confidentiality, direct communication between parties, and that they will interpret everything said in the encounter.	Performs well for the most part (introduces in both languages) but forgets to include some important pieces of information in the introduction, such as confidentiality, etc.).	Does not perform appropriately to the setting or according to the standards. Does not include important pieces of information in the introduction (confidentiality, etc.).	Does not introduce themselves as suggested by standards.
Situational management (virtual environment)	Appropriately applies communication flow management skills, successfully controlling dialogue turns. Makes appropriate and successful use of notetaking and balances between taking notes and paying attention to visual cues.	Minor hesitations, but for the most part was successful in managing the communication and turn taking. For the most part, makes appropriate and successful use of notetaking, but does not reach a balance between taking notes and paying attention to speakers, missing a few visual cues.	Some hesitations and lack of confidence in managing the flow of communication. Inappropriate use of notetaking, causing omissions and distortions of meaning. Misses important visual cues due to lack of appropriate notetaking skills.	Many hesitations and complete lack of situational management skills, causing the communication to break down. Does not make use of notes and does not ask speakers to pause in long stretches of speech, omitting important pieces of information, and producing distortions of meaning.

(Continued)

Table 5.7 (Continued)

Language	Excellent 100–90%	Good 80–70%	Fair 60–50%	Incomplete Below 50%
Clarification strategies	Successfully clarifies misunderstandings.	With few exceptions, successfully clarified misunderstandings.	Some instances of misunderstanding due to the interpreter not asking for repetition/clarification. Some omissions because of not asking parties to repeat themselves or clarifying their statements.	Many instances of misunderstanding due to the interpreter not asking for repetition/ clarification. Many omissions that caused serious distortions of meaning.
Self-check and correction of issues	Successfully corrects issues or inappropriate terms in the target language.	For the most part, corrects issues or inappropriate terms in the target language.	Some use of inappropriate terms in the target language without self-correcting.	Frequent use of inappropriate terms in the target language without self-correcting.
Professional use of camera and audio settings in teleconferencing	Lighting and space are professionally set up. Audio is clear and student is making use of headset and microphone.	For the most part lighting and space are set up in a professional manner. Student is making use of headset and microphone. However, the quality is insufficient, causing minor disruptions.	Student's face appears dark (maybe with a window behind them or inappropriate lighting). Quality of audio somewhat interferes with understanding.	Space and lighting are not set up professionally. No use of headset or microphone, interfering with communication.
TOTAL				

clarification. When you say, 'can you repeat that?,' the speaker has no idea which part of the speech you're referring to and chances are they will forget what they have said. You need to be specific when asking for repetition, 'Can you repeat the part in which you said . . .', you need to help the speaker remember the parts that you forgot. Moreover, taking notes would have helped in this situation. You ended up omitting a big chunk. You did a great job asking for clarification of 'sex drive,' and you were transparent with both speakers. Then you asked the doctor if he could say it in a different way. Great strategy. However, because you didn't take notes, you omitted what came after 'sex drive.'

Self-Checks and Corrects Mistakes: There was a big meaning distortion in your interpretation. Patient said "he follows me" and you interpreted as 'he hits me.' If you didn't hear well 'follow me' in the source language or didn't know the meaning, you should have asked the speaker to repeat. Because you were trying to figure out, and thus adding an extra effort (stress) in your brain, you omitted the next phrase when patient said, 'but I know that he loves me.'

Professional Use of Camera and Audio Settings: Because in VRI the interpreter is usually on camera, make sure you are aware of your body language and facial expressions. There was a moment when you were searching for the appropriate translation for a specific phrase and your facial expression demonstrated you were struggling and looked confused. You need to find a balance between taking notes and looking at the speakers to pick up on visual cues. Participants could barely see your face in this interaction; the room was too dark. Audio and image quality are extremely important, so always check to see if you have enough lighting in the space; if your room is messy (yes, that's important too!)."

5.6 Language Reviewers for Multilingual Translation & Interpreting Courses

For various reasons discussed previously, skills-building language-neutral courses are growing exponentially around the world, and, since instructors do not speak all languages used by their students in the classroom, so is the need for language reviewers. The rationale behind naming them reviewers and not graders has to do with the fact that in the United States, only faculty members can grade their students' work, something that is not relegated to external graders because they have no affiliation with the institution—usually independent contractors and/or vendors—and they are not aware of other graded items (written papers, reflections, quizzes, etc.) students engage with in their learning journeys. The authors acknowledge that this practice might be different in other institutions and geographic areas, but even if instructors decide to ask reviewers to suggest a grade for their students' work, the final grading should always be done by the teacher assigned to the course—grades suggested by reviewers should only be used to gauge students' language conversion strategies and proficiency levels. Another important recommendation when using language reviewers in language-neutral courses is to not allow students to connect with them directly, since this would create a relationship that is beyond the classroom with an external provider, who is not usually compensated for work that is outside their contractual obligations. Moreover, reviewers should be encouraged to anonymize their feedback and comments since students would likely be able to find information about them online and try to reach out.

5.6.1 Who Are They?

Ideally, language reviewers should be themselves experienced translators and/or interpreters in the student's language pair, preferably having taken translation and/or interpreting classes, or pursued certificates or completed graduate level studies. However, the reality in multilingual classes, which actually mirrors the reality of the professional world, is that they come from very diverse backgrounds. In courses where students are working with minority languages or languages of lesser diffusion, finding competent reviewers can be overwhelming, but not impossible. One way to overcome that is to establish strong relationships with local immigrant communities and non-profit organizations working with multicultural populations, and to leverage instructors' professional, academic, and personal networks around the world. For instance, one of the authors of this book, after an extensive search, was able to find a very good Burmese reviewer and experienced translator and interpreter, working at a local community center who agreed to provide feedback to their student. In another example referring to a recent surge of immigration from the Karen ethnicity to Minnesota, United States (discussed in Chapter 1), one of the authors was not able to identify a competent Karen reviewer in the country to provide feedback to Karen students taking online translation and interpreting courses. The solution was to look elsewhere in the world where different waves of immigration from the same ethnicity took place earlier, in the hope of finding Karen nationals who had already gone through translation and interpreter training. The instructor's academic network eventually led him to a university in Australia. The Royal Melbourne Institute of Technology (RMIT) is one of the largest training providers in Australia and, since 1975, has been training interpreters and translators in many community languages. These range from established ones such as Arabic, Chinese, Greek, Japanese, Italian, Korean, Vietnamese, and Turkish, to more recent and emerging languages such as Burmese, Dari, Dinka, Tamil, and Karen. Through a wonderful and generous colleague, who at the time headed the educational programs at RMIT, well-known translation and interpreting educator and scholar Miranda Lai, one of the authors of this book was introduced to a Karen graduate of the RMIT interpreting diploma. After a few email exchanges,

Waan Tardiff, who lives in Australia, became the language reviewer for our Karen students in the United States.

One of the many challenges that arises in this collaboration is the issue of equitable feedback to all students since the diversity in the background of language reviewers can present issues. One way to address that is first to have a clear idea of what one wants in the form of feedback from language reviewers (examples are offered in Chapter 4), which for the most part should be done in the pivot language of the program—English, in the case of the authors of this book. Another piece of advice is to have meetings or email exchanges with reviewers before the start of the semester to clarify expectations and share examples of excellent feedback. This can be easily done using any videoconference tools such as Zoom; such meetings can also be recorded and made available to reviewers who are not able to attend due to different time zones.

Notes

1 https://learn.echo360.com/hc/en-us/articles/360047228731-Creating-a-Poll
2 Contrasting with the more commonly used language of "students are required," or "students must," etc., the authors of this book have moved to using more inclusive and welcoming language as proposed by the UDL framework, discussed in Chapter 1.

References

Altman, Jane. "Error Analysis in the Teaching of Simultaneous Interpreting." *Bridging the Gap: Empirical Research in Simultaneous Interpretation*, edited by Barbara Moser-Mercer and Sylvie Lambert. John Benjamins Publishing Company, 1994.

Anderson, L.W., et al. *A Taxonomy for Learning, Teaching, and Assessing: A Revision of Bloom's Taxonomy of Educational Objectives*. Longman, 2001.

Badalotti, Floriana. "Can You Translate into Your L2?" *Academic Language Experts*, 15 Mar. 2019, www.aclang.com/blog/can-you-translate-into-your/.

Bartlomiejczyk, Magdalena. "Interpreting Quality as Perceived by Trainee Interpreters." *The Interpreter and Translator Trainer*, vol. 1, 2007, pp. 247–67.

Chernov, Ghelly V. "Message Redundancy and Message Anticipation in Simultaneous Interpretation." *Bridging the Gap: Empirical Research in Simultaneous Interpretation*, edited by Barbara Moser-Mercer and Sylvie Lambert. John Benjamins Publishing Company, 1994.

Chesterman, Andrew, and Emma Wagner. *Can Theory Help Translators? A Dialogue between the Ivory Tower and the Wordface*. Routledge, 2014.

Choi, Jung Yoon. "Metacognitive Evaluation Method in Consecutive Interpretation for Novice Learners." *Meta*, vol. 51, no. 2, June 2006, pp. 273–83.

Gile, Daniel. "Facing and Coping with Online Problems in Interpreting." *Basic Concepts and Models for Interpreter and Translator Training*, John Benjamins Publishing Company, 2009.

Jay-Rayon, Laurence Ibrahim Aibo, et al. "Three Pedagogical Tools to Take Your Online Translation and Interpreting Course to the Next Level." *The ATA Chronicle*, Feb. 2020, www.ata-chronicle.online/featured/three-pedagogical-tools-to-take-your-online-translation-and-interpreting-courses-to-the-next-level/.

Kuto, Emmanuel Kobena. "Remodelling Institutional Translation: An African Perspective." La Traduction et l'interprétation En Afrique Subsaharienne : Les Nouveaux Défis d'un Espace Multilingue / Translation and Interpretation in Sub-Saharan Africa: New Challenges in a Multilingual Space, edited by Justine Ndongo-Keller et al. Univesité Libre de Bruxelles, 2021, pp. 111–24.

Lederer, Marianne. "Simultaneous Interpretation—Units of Meaning and Other Features." *Language Interpretation and Communication*, edited by David Gerver and H. Sinaiko. NATO Conference Series, 1978, pp. 323–32.

McDonald, Danny. "Writing Discussion Forum Questions." *Wiley Education Services*, 12 Oct. 2016, https://ctl.wiley.com/writing-discussion-forum-questions/.

Musampa, Emmanuel Kambaja. "Formation du Traducteur dans le contexte multilingue de La RDC: Quelles Compétences face aux défis actuels?" *La Traduction et l'interprétation en Afrique Subsaharienne: Les Nouveaux Défis d'un Espace Multilingue/Translation and Interpretation in Sub-Saharan Africa: New Challenges in a Multilingual Space*, edited by Justine Ndongo-Keller et al., Université Libre de Bruxelles, 2021, pp. 95–110.

Parr, Tony. "The Mother-Tongue Principle: Hit or Myth." *The ATA Chronicle*, 2016, www.ata-chronicle.online/featured/the-mother-tongue-principle-hit-or-myth/.

Pokorn, N.K. "Translating into a Non-Mother Tongue in Translation Theory: Deconstruction of the Traditional." *Translation in Context*, edited by Andrew Chesterman. John Benjamins Publishing Company, 2000.

Seleskovitch, Danica. "Language and Memory: A Study of Note-Taking in Consecutive Interpreting." *The Interpreting Studies Reader*, edited by Franz Pochhacker and Miriam Shlesinger. Routledge, 2001.

Stevens, D.D., and A.J. Levi. *Introduction to Rubrics: An Assessment Tool to Save Grading Time, Convey Effective Feedback, and Promote Student Learning*. Stylus, 2012.

6 Ethics in Online Translation and Interpreting Courses

This chapter discusses why ethics should be at the core of any online translation and interpreting program, and its place in developing critical thinking and decision-making in applied settings. As stated in Chapter 5, the authors strongly believe that teaching T&I as situated, culturally and socially anchored activities is essential and inseparable from teaching T&I as applied activities. Helping students become educated critical thinkers allows them to become reflective practitioners, capable of pondering about their own practice and their impact on others, but also on the realities of translation and interpreting around them. We would also like to suggest that ethics should not be solely taught in a designated ethics course. Rather, we believe that ethics should be addressed in multiple ways, ranging from:

- readings focused on ethics while addressing other topics (such as dilemmas for courthouse interpreters)
- short subunits embedded in weekly learning modules across all courses, for instance in a medical interpretation course or an introduction to translation one
- dedicated module(s) on ethics embedded in another course, for instance "translation technology"
- a full-blown course dedicated to T&I ethics, which can include hands-on T&I assignments, as will be illustrated in this chapter

While teaching ethics does rely on engaging students with sometimes demanding readings, envisioning ethics as an integral part of any given T&I course avoids isolating ethics from practitioners' activities and presenting it as a purely intellectual or theoretical exercise. This argument has already been made at the beginning of Chapter 5 with a reference to Chesterman and Wagner's book (*Can Theory Help Translators? A Dialogue Between the Ivory Tower and the Wordface*), and more specifically with a reference to Chesterman's convincing argument regarding the intrinsic "correlations between cause and effect [that] should be part of a professional's awareness" (2014, 5–6).

DOI: 10.4324/9781003149316-7

It is helpful to introduce William Perry's (1968) scaffolded model of ethical development to guide students through those stages, from lowest to highest:

- *Duality*: Knowledge is divided into right and wrong; knowledge is absolute, it is handed down from authorities, and learned passively; the view of knowledge is *quantitative* (163).
- *Multiplicity*: Knowledge is a question of opinion; evaluation is seen as subjective; student prone to frustration if one's own perspective not validated; student entertains differences of opinion, no longer absolute "rightness"; learning becomes personal, knowledge constructed (164).
- *Relativism*: Knowledge shifts toward a qualitative view of knowledge. Not all opinions are equally valid. Rather than sages, instructors now become guides and model critical engagement with content. Student is still frustrated that no theory is all-embracing (164).
- *Commitment*: Knowledge is now nuanced and informed. The student commits to a theory not as an absolute but as a foundation for further refinement (165).

Some of the components of a T&I ethics course may include the following ones:

- raising students' awareness of the impact of the work of translators and interpreters on the lives of other people
- helping students reflect on the statuses and livelihood of translators and interpreters around the world and how those are impacted by changes in the global economy
- exposing students to a variety of situations and settings, such as dilemmas, conflicts, war, migration, immigration, and border crisis
- engaging students with the problematic and insufficiently discussed ethical implications of machine translation
- introducing students to service learning, volunteering and their many ethical ramifications
- introducing notions of race and privilege in translation
- preparing students to navigate power dynamics and the assumptions of visibility vs. invisibility in interpreting encounters
- more generally, preparing students for the unexpected and equipping them with solid conceptual tools and critical thinking skills

6.1 The Impact of the Work of Translators and Interpreters on the Lives of Other People

Mona Baker calls for ethics to be at the center of translation and interpreting education, reminding us that the professional side of both tasks has traditionally perceived translators and interpreters as "apolitical professionals whose priority is to earn a living by serving the needs of their fee paying clients" (2015), and so have many educational programs available to students. However, practitioners, in recent years, have started to challenge this perception of the profession by offering their views on a range of issues and engaging with ethical implications of their work.

One such high-profile professional is Erik Camayd-Freixas, a federally certified Spanish interpreter who has openly criticized the United States Federal Court System in their handling of immigration issues. His article "Interpreting after the Largest ICE Raid in US History: A Personal Account," (2009) is often quoted as an example of a professional interpreter voicing their concern about injustice. In this particular case, Camayd-Freixas sheds light on how the legal system criminalized undocumented immigrants who were arrested at a meatpacking plant in the State of Iowa in 2008. By forcing them to plead guilty to the charge of identity theft, even though most of the workers had no idea what a social security number was and were given such numbers by their employers, the court presented the option as a way for them to spend less time in jail and be deported back to their home countries. After the case was closed, Camayd-Freixas described major abuses these immigrant workers had to endure. Although accused of breaking the ethical principle of confidentiality, in a polemical *New York Times* article (Preston 2008) Camayd-Freixas insisted he had not:

> The interpreter code of ethics, in particular the clause of confidentiality, has as its meaning and rationale that the interpreter must *not influence the outcome of the case*. The Postville case had been closed, and its 10-day deadline for appeal had expired before I even began the essay. I do not mention any names and aside from anecdotal information of a general nature, all the facts mentioned are either in the public record or freely available on the Internet. So I was careful not to break the code of confidentiality.
>
> Moreover, confidentiality is not absolute. There are other ethical requirements which override confidentiality. For example, a medical interpreter, in whom a patient confides that he has an epidemic disease, has the obligation to report it because it is in the public interest to do so. Similarly, in the Postville case, there were higher imperatives arising not only out of public interest but also out of the legal role of the court interpreter.
>
> (Camayd-Freixas 2008)

This high-profile case study, which aptly illustrates a consequentialist ethics, is one of the many that can be introduced in the T&I ethics classroom, not only from the perspective of dilemmas, but also to illustrate advocacy work. As Camayd-Freixas rightly states, confidentiality is not absolute, and ethical principles, both professional and personal ones, often collide with each other. Dilemmas are actually part and parcel of community interpreters' daily work. It is therefore essential to introduce codes of ethics as guidelines and not as a series of rigid principles set in stone, but rather as starting point for examining, discussing, and challenging them.

Ethical dilemmas, albeit more frequent and immediate in interpreters' lives, are also real for translators. Terena Bell, then head of a translation agency based in Kentucky, points out real situations her company was faced with:

> If Blackwater asked you to translate assembly instructions for an automatic rifle, would you do it? What if they told you the document's target audience was teenagers in the Sudan? This is not a hypothetical, but a real dilemma my staff had to grapple with a few years ago.
>
> Military contracts and contractors aside, the language services profession is replete with controversial issues. If you're pro-life, do you interpret for an abortion clinic? If you're pro-choice, do you interpret for a crisis pregnancy center? And it doesn't stop there. Legal interpreters who are against the death penalty may have to interpret judgments they don't agree with, and feminist translators are asked to localize for adult entertainment.
>
> (Bell 2010, 41)

Such dilemmas are even more insidious when they arise from clients who usually send content that does not require any ethical decision-making. One of the authors was faced with a delicate situation when one of their regular clients sent them a military-related translation project that was in sharp contrast with the usual humanities projects sent by them. Students can advantageously discuss this kind of case studies in their weekly discussion space and generate lists of questions, starting with a very broad one: How should/could one respond? Reactions could encompass radical ones, which would have the translator stop working with this particular client based on their ideological stance, or more temperate ones, where the translator would simply inform their client of the type of content they are not willing to engage with. In their discussion (or other assignment type), students might also realize that the decision may be contingent on the nature of the past and usual projects sent by the client. Such ethical dilemmas do not fall within the ones covered by professional codes of ethics and standards of practice. In fact, many ethical dilemmas pertaining to the potentially problematic content of a translation or topic of an interpreting assignment transcend ethical principles or tenets or require such tenets to be challenged, which is a desirable outcome in the T&I classroom. Additionally, students need to be able to frame dilemmas within individual morals and values.

In an ethics class, more than in any other classes, reflections accompanying translation and interpreting assignments play an essential role. Controversial topics or situations in translation and interpreting settings need to be framed in specific contexts, with specific audiences, and specific objectives.

Baker discusses how "ethical decisions must be *situated*," and illustrates her point with the following example.

> For instance, the decision as to whether it is ethically responsible to interpret for a far right speaker like Jean-Marie Le Pen of the French National Front Party, as Clare Donovan and her ESIT students concluded after much discussion, could depend on the venue of the speech. Many students, and Clare Donovan herself, considered it unethical to interpret for Le Pen in a rally attended by his supporters, since this would help him promote his ideology in a context in which it would not be challenged. Interpreting a speech by Le Pen at the European Union, on the other hand, can be defended on ethical grounds since many delegates who can and arguably should challenge him in such a venue first need to understand what views he is advocating as accurately as possible.
>
> (2015, n. pag.)

T&I assignments in an ethics class may focus on controversial topics such as weaponry, abortion, vulnerable communities' rights, or extremist ideologies, to name but a few. The authors like to ask their students to imagine their own settings, audiences, and purpose(s) for their own translation or interpretation assignments when writing their reflections. Although essential, imagining a specific audience and the impact of their translation or interpretation on such an audience is an exercise that is challenging for some students, yet crucial to making an informed decision as to whether accept or decline a project. Modeling and showcasing exemplars of audience descriptions from past semesters is a good idea.

To help students engage in critical thinking, it is important to introduce fundamental conceptual tools to equip them for ethical discussions. Baker distinguishes the teleological approach, which essentially focuses on immediate consequences, and the deontological one, which prioritizes human dignity as an essential value, notwithstanding the impact of one's decision on participants in a translation project of interpreting encounter.

> **Deontological** models define what is ethical by reference to what is right in and of itself, irrespective of consequences, and are rule-based. **Teleological** approaches, on the other hand, define what is ethical by reference to what produces the best results. Utilitarianism . . . is a teleological theory that is more concerned with consequences than with what is morally right *per se*.
>
> (Baker 2015)

While more specific conceptual models can be introduced as needed in the T&I ethics classroom such as Drugan and Tipton's social responsibility (2017) or Hoza's interpreter sensibility model (2003), introducing deontological and teleological approaches early in the semester is a good idea to help students start debating from different perspectives. A basic exercise consists of asking a group of students to analyze a case study based on the deontological model, while asking another group to use the teleological perspective, then to compare their respective approaches in their weekly discussion space. This can be done on rich media content discussion platforms such as VoiceThread, as illustrated in more detail in Chapter 4.

Discussion forums/blogs/spaces or weekly discussions, depending on their frequency and what instructors prefer to call them, are an essential part of any course devoted to or any module focusing on T&I ethics. A good mix of various professional codes of ethics from different countries, theoretical readings, articles in T&I industry magazines focused on professional practice, and a section that could be named "ethics in the news," with papers such as Chris Bell's (2017) "Iranian Interpreter Defends Trump Speech Omissions," published on BBC news, or the more recent publication eloquently illustrating ambiguity in translation and ethical dilemmas in the court house pertaining to a poorly translated DNA consent form by Massachusetts State Police (Cote 2021), allows students to immediately understand the multiple and close connections between theory and practice. Articulating theoretical concepts to concrete cases covered in the news has proved very successful, from the point of view of meeting learning objectives and engaging students with more complex theoretical readings, in the T&I Ethics class taught by one of the authors. Readings should be enriched with curated webinars, documentaries (see *Justice in Translation* mentioned in one of the assignments presented at the end of this chapter), and even works of fiction (see *Day One* or *Un Traductor* mentioned later) that yield themselves to discussing ethics in a highly engaging way.

6.2 Statuses and Livelihood of Translators and Interpreters Around the World: How are those Impacted by Changes in the Global Economy?

Changes in the global economy and legal loopholes have recently brought up a heavily debated topic: rates and livelihood of translators and interpreters across the globe. Moorkens points out how the global recession that started around 2008 increased precarity, undermined the agency of translators, and accelerated a "downward pressure on costs and productivity," while "continued growth has been reported for the language industry" (Moorkens 2017, 464). At the beginning of 2021, a large interpretation services company contracting with New York City Public Schools and New York Health + Hospitals, the largest public health care system in the United States, received press coverage after former interpreters based in Mexico claimed receiving as little as $4 an hour whereas the minimum wage is $15 an hour in New York City (*Multilingual* 2021; Elsen-Rooney 2021; Chew 2021). Other issues such as insufficient training and inadequate confidentiality measures were also raised by former employees and relayed by the media. Such news can and should be used as a case study to debate the vexed issue of rates and working conditions in an increasingly globalized world, where ethical and legal questions overlap (what is legal is not always ethical or is at least highly debatable from an ethical perspective.)

Students can apply the teleological and deontological approaches, but also social responsibility to discuss this topic. Insufficient rates should be discussed from both a global and local perspective, and the debate should also address the status of the profession as a whole. Such discussions can take place after students have been introduced to the fundamental characteristics of a profession (AALEP 2016), for example. Beginners and non-professional translators and interpreters alike fail to acknowledge how harmful accepting low rates is to the profession, which already struggles for adequate recognition, while "low" is also a relative notion that can be based on a variety of criteria (make a living, feed one's family, live a comfortable life, belong to middle-income households, etc.). This debate can adequately be tied to Baker's discussion on volunteerism, which points to the "growing tendency for non-profit and humanitarian organisations to solicit free translation and interpreting from students, who are often happy to undertake the work in order to gain experience and boost their CVs" (Baker 2015, n. pag.). As we argue later in this chapter, we also believe, like Jerez et al., that "managed judiciously and in the appropriate contexts, volunteerism in the case of translation and interpreting can be an ethical and socially responsible choice" (Manuel Jerez et al. 2004, quoted in Baker 2015). Volunteerism can also be approached from a completely different perspective, as a means for recent immigrants to be socialized, valued, and recognized in their own rights as Aguilar-Solano (2015) aptly demonstrated with the example of volunteer immigrant interpreters in Southern Spain hospitals.

A completely different and very disturbing practice is the increasing trend observed with large digital media corporations asking for free translations. This phenomenon, for lack of a better terminology, needs to be seriously discussed in the ethics classroom. As pointed out by Baker analyzing Twitter's Translation Agreement, this is a growing and concerning tendency that is curiously insufficiently addressed in the classroom. The following is the first section of said "agreement" as presented by Baker:

Translation Agreement

Terms and conditions **do** apply. Step 1 of 2.

Overview

Since you'll be helping out Twitter (thanks again!) we want to let you know our ground rules. Please read the full agreement below before continuing. Here are some of the things you can expect to see:

- We may show you confidential, yet to be released products or features and you must be willing to **keep those secret**.

- You'll be **volunteering** to help out Twitter and will not be paid.
- Twitter **owns the rights** to the translations you provide. You are **giving** them to us so that we can use them however we want.

Among other things, Twitter plans to **share the translations** with the Twitter development community. We want to help make all of the other great Twitter apps, not just Twitter.com, available in your language.

Baker (2015, n. pag.)

Students will benefit from engaging in a discussion on the consequences of free translations for the profession as a whole since digital giants are by no means organizations with limited financial means, nor are NGOs. As mentioned earlier, the section dedicated to volunteerism and service learning in this chapter will suggest a variety options for students to develop their skills in a real-world setting.

6.3 Ethical Implications of Machine Translation

An insufficiently addressed topic in the T&I ethics classroom pertains to ethical considerations of machine translation. The authors believe that a module on MT ethics should be part of both translation technology courses and ethics courses, as briefly hinted at in the section on artificial intelligence in Chapter 1 ("Should MT be part of an ethics course?"). Relatively little has been published on the ethics of translation technology, although recent blog post authors (Love 2019; Pilinu 2019) are starting to raise more specific questions about machine translation (stated in Bowker 2021).

Addressing the ethical implications of MT to students can start with notions of privacy breaches, which presupposes introducing MT and AI and their multiple applications in people's everyday lives. For instance, most students ignore that free MT tools are associated with potential breaches of confidentiality. Free MT tools do not guarantee privacy of the content being copied and pasted into their platform. And free MT comes in many forms, including the automatic translation feature embedded in Microsoft Office Word. In 2017, *Slator* reported a massive privacy breach involving a free MT tool whose terms and conditions stated that while the company:

> "will use reasonable measures to protect any content you provide to us for the purpose of completing the Services," they "cannot and do not guarantee that any information provided to us by you will not become public under any circumstances. You should appreciate that all information submitted on the website might potentially be publicly accessible."
>
> (Faes 2017)

With the advent of free online MT tools such as Google Translate in the early 2000s, the general public started using translation technology (Bowker 2021) without understanding its ethical and legal implications (who reads Google's Terms & Conditions, especially the fine lines?) Bowker rightly points out that free online MT tools are nowadays embedded in many other software solutions and therefore increase inadvertent privacy breaches:

> For instance, users may imagine that the data entered into a free online MT service simply disappears once the translation process is completed. However, MT service providers are typically interested in keeping this data and in possibly reusing it in the future (e.g., as training data). As the capacity and availability of free MT tools expand, so too will the amount of inadvertently disclosed sensitive data.
> (Bowker 2021, 266)

Another important ethical consideration related to translation technology in general, including MT, CAT Tools, and Translation Memories (TMs), pertains to the ownership of translated content, which is indissociable from the commoditization of translation.[1] As pointed out by Bowker (2021) referring to Moorkens and Lewis (2020), translators find themselves in copyright conundrums and legal loopholes:

> While translators do have legal rights and copyright ownership of both target texts and aligned TM databases, translation industry employment practices often make it challenging for translators to assert their rights. What's more, the lawyers who drafted the copyright legislation did not predict that translations would go on to be reused to such a large extent, whether in TM tools or as MT training data. Parallel corpus data is now being repurposed in ever-increasing amounts, but broken down to word and even sub-word levels, which are not clearly covered by copyright legislation. Although copyright law continues to evolve, Moorkens and Lewis (2020) note that, to date, there has been no significant impact on the reality of translation data ownership: many freelance translators still feel pressure to hand over their TM databases to agencies or clients because not doing so might affect the translator's standing with that service provider and cause payment problems.
> (Bowker 2021, 266)

McDonough Dolmaya (2011) found out that codes of ethics from large professional T&I associations around the globe did not cover the ethical use of translation technology. As we write these lines in 2021, this observation is still true, although professional organizations have now started thinking about adding a section on MT in their codes of ethics. Instructors should address this worrying gap with their students and examine codes of ethics in a critical way, pointing out their shortcomings: "some educators have been slow to provide students with the deep understanding of ethical issues that is now called for in this highly technologized profession" (Bowker 2021, 273).

Kenny and Doherty (2014) and Kenny (2020) (quoted in Bowker 2021) urge instructors to address ethical considerations related to technology as part of T&I education and Bowker points out that "there is a need for technology-related ethics to be addressed more systematically across the curriculum (Bowker 2021, 273).

Additional issues linked to translation technology include attacks to large neural machine translation systems, as explained in a July 2021 *Slator* article. Attackers "can manipulate MT systems quite easily to produce specific, malicious output, such as misinformation or slander" (Albarino 2021, n. pag.) on a very large scale and can damage specific targets together with the reputation of translation providers (who may face legal consequences). The University of Melbourne in Australia, together with digital media giants, released a paper on that worrying topic in July 2021 (Wang et al. 2021). In the summer of 2021, we do not have sufficient perspective to envision how to specifically address, beyond assigning readings on the topic, these recent MT issues with students in the T&I ethics classroom or from an ethical perspective in the translation technology classroom. However, it seems fitting to link them with Michael Cronin's critique of translation technology from an environmental perspective in the sense that there is greater need for storage of large databases as technologies advance, which leads to increased consumption of energy. Such MT data centers require more energy than other, less advanced industries, producing enormous amounts of heat, which in turn need to be cooled down. "There is nothing immaterial about the material consequences of virtual technologies," argues Cronin (2019, 520), while suggesting such data hubs are major contributors to climate change. The range of assignments that can be envisioned on that topic starts with online student-led discussions, to live (synchronous) or recorded (asynchronous) classroom presentations, up to capstone or final projects.

Another ethical concern about MT is its capacity to reproduce, amplify, and systematize gender biases when translating from a non-gender marked language to a gender marked one. Short, apparently simplistic MT exercises with textual content such as the following excerpts can be designed to help students assess potential gender biases perpetuated by MT tools when translating from a non-gender marked source language such as English, to gender marked target languages such as Romance languages. Needless to state that much more sophisticated content can be selected for full-fledged assignments.

"You can become an engineer, a physician or doctor, a physicist, or a researcher.
You can become a nurse.
You can become an aid.
You can become a truck driver."

As we write these lines, we are fully aware that the issue of gender biases might at some point become a thing of the past, but at the same time, we strongly believe that additional issues will appear and that students will increasingly need solid education about the varied consequences of MT, as opposed to training on the use of MT only, as is the case across many existing translation curricula.

6.4 Finding Practice Spaces Outside of Class

6.4.1 Community Engagement and Service Learning

While thinking about ways to provide translation and interpreting students with opportunities to develop their skills outside the classroom environment—what Ineke Creeze calls "semi-authentic practices" (2015, 50)—both authors of this book were introduced to the theoretical frameworks and applications of community engagement and service learning (CESL) in higher education through different 2018–2019 fellowships promoted by their institutions. The programs included monthly meetings between faculty members—from different colleges and departments—and facilitators, with discussions of readings, sharing of engaging exercises, conversations about assessment, students' reflections, and a final project selected by the participants. Ideas for final projects included creating a new CESL-designated course, reviewing existing courses to include CESL, or engaging with different types of community outreach programs, workshops, etc. A straightforward definition of the concept can be found in a report by the Center for Service Learning and Civic Engagement department of Michigan State University,

> Service Learning is a teaching method that combines academic coursework with the application of institutional resources (e.g., knowledge and expertise of students, faculty and staff, political position, buildings and land) to address challenges facing communities through collaboration with these communities. This pedagogy focuses on critical, reflective thinking to develop students' academic skills, sense of civic responsibility, and commitment to the community.
>
> (2015, n.d., 1)

For those unfamiliar with this framework, the origin of CESL in the United States is very intertwined with volunteerism, the Civil Rights Movement, and the War on Poverty program—dating back to the 1960s and 1970s—which focused on the "community involvement in the Peace Corps, VISTA, the Senior Companion Program, Habitat for Humanity, and several worthwhile, industrious programs" (Los Angeles County Office of Education n.d., 1). Currently, the more common approaches to service learning (SL) include traditional SL, critical SL, and liberating SL, as defined in the following discussion.

Traditional SL is focused on service to the community, preparing students for civic engagement after college, and includes a consideration of the activity as a reciprocal process where both the receiver and provider of the service benefit equally. Critical SL proposes an ongoing reflection about the experience, in which students see themselves as agents of social change and service aims at addressing and responding to injustice. Liberating SL entails a stronger focus on organizing for social change stemming from educated constituents and facilitated by academics and students (Correa & Krupczynski 2018/2019, 2).

There are two major camps today in CESL scholarship. With the publication of the *Cambridge Handbook of Service Learning and Community Engagement*, it becomes clear that one of the factions is very much focused on the liberating framework mentioned previously, through statements such as,

> for too long the commodification of higher education has created the student-consumer identity and turned faculty and staff into college concierges while students get along with the more important part of their degree completion—career training and development and job placement.
>
> (Dolgon, Mitchel, and Eatman 2018, xviii)

Calling for SL practitioners to work against oppression in all its manifestations, the group argues that participants "must be willing to take on the big questions of democracy and political engagement" (2018, xix). The other group subscribes to a more nuanced view of CESL, one that takes into account the realities of our lives as educators, "ensconced within a neoliberal age, trying desperately . . . to teach our classes, engage our students, uplift our communities" (Sarofian-Butin 2017, 165), which the authors of this book subscribe to. Of course, we all want to fight oppression and make real changes in the world around us, but such transformations can also be achieved through small actions that have actual impact on people's lives, even if they cannot be easily quantified. Another important thing to bear in mind is that CESL should be seen in a continuum between social justice and change on one end, and meaningful internship, practicum, and practice opportunities for students on the other. Moreover, service learning "provides a unique situated learning experience that allows students to participate in a 'community of practice,' learning by immersion and not just by internalizing knowledge" (Acedo 2017, 51). Instructors interested in using the CESL framework in their translation and interpreting courses should take into account a host of different elements, including the particularities of students, the communities served and their needs, and colleges and universities offering the courses.

Currently, one will find centers for civic engagement and service learning in almost any university or college in the United States, with students connecting to community organizations and non-profits and working and serving in different projects connected to their academic courses and studies.

For online translation and interpreting courses, the most obvious partners to connect students with are organizations that provide service and assistance to immigrant communities in different places both locally and around the world.

Lessons Learned From a CESL-Designated T&I Course

Service learning is a major component in an introductory translation and interpreting course taught by one of the authors of this book. After several iterations of the class, some suggestions for instructors who want to expose their students to this framework while providing them with opportunities for practice include:

- Connect with your academic institution for resources, or, if not affiliated with a college or university, conduct research on the topic, which is widely available for public use on the Internet.
- Use your own networks, and others' (including your academic institution's), to select community organizations and non-profits that are interested in working with your students. Meet with your partners over the phone or videoconference to discuss concepts, expectations, etc. Chances are they do not understand much about translation and interpreting as professional activities and will appreciate learning about them as well.
- Have a clear description of what kind of services students can engage in with partners and share them with everyone involved. Obviously, students can work on translation and interpreting assignments for immigrant populations served by the organization, but in multilingual classes there might not be a demand or need for the students' language pair among the selected partners. In this particular instance, two alternative solutions can be offered to students:

    1   Students can be asked to find their own community/non-profit partners, connecting instructors with someone in charge of the organization so that they can establish rapport and manage the partner's expectations regarding such services.
    2   Expand the list of services beyond translation and interpreting to include: building or refining specialized glossaries in different languages; exploring the extent of translated materials or interpreter services available at the organization's website or materials; designing and/or conducting surveys for the organization (including interpreter client satisfaction survey, translation/interpreting client needs, etc.); developing tool kits for training of translators/ interpreters or for building awareness among users of translation/ interpreting; administrative projects that involve scheduling of interpreters; writing scripts for answering calls from non-English speakers; helping to organize interpreted events; and other tasks defined by the organization. Even if not practicing translation and

interpreting skills per se, students learn so much about clients' needs, how language mediation activities are perceived by the partner and their audience, the complexities of scheduling, procuring, and commissioning T&I work, etc.

- Expose and engage students with CESL framework readings, in particular, articles that address the concept of serving. One recommendation is the very short "Helping, Fixing, or Serving?" by Naomi Remen (2017), in which the author suggests serving as a concept that strengthens all stakeholders involved in the relationship. Another recommendation is to assign a couple of chapters from *Community Translation*, by Taibi & Ozolins, which, even though the book is focused on written translation, provides students with a deeper understanding of language brokering in such community settings, characterized "by power asymmetries," and suggests that such cultural mediation hopefully "contributes to redressing" them (2016, 13).
- Include a paragraph in the course syllabus reminding students that those community organizations and non-profits are generally understaffed, underfunded, and sometimes become overwhelmed by the many expectations that service learning requires. Students should remember that such understanding should permeate their relationship with their partners and that communication might be slower, feedback might not be available for their service, etc.
- Alert students to the importance of asking permission from their partners to add anything to their resumes regarding the service they performed during the experience, and avoid creating a false impression of "professional experience."
- Depending on the length of the course, include at least two reflective assignments in the course (journals or blogs)—one in the beginning and another near the end—so that instructors can provide feedback and intervene if any additional support is needed or if corrections in the relationship or service must be made. In general, a final project is expected, in which students will present their CESL experience online to the entire class, connecting it to T&I concepts and knowledge acquired in class. Such activity can also include a document with suggestions to the partner on how they can better serve their immigrant communities.
- If possible, meet synchronously with students, at least twice for semester-long courses, to follow their progress and address any questions they may have.
- The recommendation, at least in the institution where one of the authors currently teaches, is that students should spend a maximum of 20 hours per semester on CESL, since they have to dedicate time to other academic course requirements (T&I assignments, quizzes, online discussions of articles, etc.).

As one can see from these recommendations, CESL requires a lot of dedication and involvement by instructors, both with establishing and managing contacts with community organizations and following up on students' commitment and progress. On the other hand, projects can be built into the course load in a way to make sure there is a balance among everyone's time commitment to service learning. For example, in the course taught by one of the authors, the number of articles read for class was reduced, as well as the number of T&I assignments. As stated by Acedo, "it is important to highlight that service learning represents a significant component of the syllabus, teaching activities and assignments, and the grade students obtain in a certain course" (2017, 53–4).

6.4.2 Pre-Professional Collaborations Within and Across Institutions

Another way to provide students with spaces for safe practice and improve their skills outside of class includes interprofessional partnerships. While several other professional degrees, including health care, law, etc., include pre-professional experiences—some of them in simulated environments—as mandatory components of their curriculum, except for sporadic and individual attempts by educators and institutions (Crezee 2015; Acedo 2017), translation and interpreting has been slow in incorporating similar educational practices in a systemic way. Since translators and interpreters will go out into the world after training and interact with different professions as language mediators, it makes sense to expose students to "semi-authentic practices." Such experiences provide opportunities for them to perform under conditions closer to those they will encounter in their future professional lives, in addition to developing "an underlying understanding of genres and socio-pragmatic norms" (Crezee 2015, 52). The same is true for nurses, doctors, lawyers, social workers, teachers, etc., who will invariably interact with speakers of other languages, so why not bring students from both programs together to develop the skills they will need in their future careers? Such collaborations can be done within institutions—as in connecting T&I courses with the nursing department's simulation exercises, international journalism courses, criminal justice students, etc.—and across different colleges and universities, which is exemplified in the following example.

One of the authors of this book networked and collaborated with professors from the University of Minnesota School of Dentistry while working at a different institution to design workshops and train dental students on how to work with interpreters. The objectives defined for the oral health students by their faculty were twofold: to improve the quality of oral healthcare to limited English proficient (LEP) patients, and to develop the skills of working effectively with spoken language interpreters. For interpreting students, the goals included improving their performance through pre-professional practice and becoming familiar with oral care contexts and terminology. The collaborative project started in 2016 as in-person workshops and simulated practice (Quick et al. 2019), morphed into a hybrid format in 2018, and became a fully online experience during the COVID-19 pandemic, made possible by a videoconference platform (Zoom). Students from both programs received feedback from the instructors, experts, facilitators present in the different sessions, and more importantly, from each other, thus creating a community of learners. One dental student commented about learning from their interpreting colleagues that, "they definitely had a chance to give feedback to us, which is very good, which never happens in a clinical setup. Normally they will never talk to you about how you're dealing with them" (Quick et al. 2019, 651). As a result of this research project, and very much in line with the interactive interpretation framework proposed by Cecilia Wadensjö, in which "the dynamics of the interaction will largely depend on the socio-cultural conventions associated with the type of situation (in institutional terms) in the which the interpreting occurs, and on participants' respective understanding of what it means to speak via an interpreter," (1999, 154), "working effectively with interpreters" is now considered a skill to be developed by the School of Dentistry students, currently embedded in their curriculum (Woll et al. 2020). Moreover, with the understanding that "simulation is a key educational strategy that allows interprofessional training . . . providing individuals with opportunities to practice working together, apply knowledge and processes, develop relationships, break down disciplinary silos, and work to provide patient-center care," such collaboration has also produced a curriculum—publicly available online—which can be replicated by other institutions or programs (Woll et al. 2020, n. pag.).

The simulated interpreted encounters in later iterations of the project on Zoom have also allowed interpreting students to further develop their skills in the new virtual environment brought about by technological changes and exacerbated by the COVID-19 worldwide pandemic, learning to manage remote interpreted dialogues. Based on observations of the online interprofessional practice performed by students, some of the takeaways for interpreting students in the context of remote dialogue interpreting include the following observations:

- In monolingual appointments, providers and institutions control the communication. In bilingual appointments, they need to negotiate power with the interpreter, who is the only person with access to both languages and cultures, so having a quick pre-session to establish turn-taking conventions and interpreting mode to be used, whether speakers need to pause more frequently, and other professional standards for dialogue interpreter (principles of transparency, first person usage, etc.) is advisable.
- Making proper introductions before interpretation begins to set up expectations of all participants is crucial.

- If interpreters do not yet master note-taking for consecutive interpretation, they need to find a strategy to manage turn taking (request shorter sentences, hand gestures to request pauses, etc.).
- As part of managing the flow of communication (e.g., in a remote environment, sound gets cut off when speakers are talking on top of each other), interpreters should request that speakers wait until interpretation is finished (turn taking conventions).
- In VRI (video remote interpreting), audio and image quality are extremely important, so interpreters always need to check if they have enough lighting in the space; if their room is tidy (yes, that's important too!); if their face does not appear too dark; and if they have adequate equipment (headset and microphone).
- In VRI, because of audio being cut off when two voices overlap, there is no need to interpret simple answers that have universal meaning, such as "OK," "yes," etc., especially when they are followed by non-verbal cues (nodding, etc.).
- Interpreters need to balance between the need to take notes and look at the camera to pick up on visual cues.
- Interpreters need to be aware of their own facial expressions when interpreting on video, especially when they're struggling with finding translations for words or phrases.
- Everyone in the interaction needs to be aware of bandwidth and implications for their video and sound connections.

Again, similar to CESL, this type of collaboration within and across institutions does involve a lot of planning and commitment and T&I educators must decide if it is worth getting involved with in terms of their scope of work, their employment relationships with institutions, etc. However, one thing is sure, such type of pre-professional practice and simulated scenarios are excellent opportunities for students to develop their interpreting and performance skills, prepare for their professional lives, and develop a deeper understanding about translation and interpreting as cultural and social activities. As one interpreting student put it, "the fact that we're all students practicing how to handle a real medical situation offered me the opportunity to see and check my performance as an interpreter. . . . This is something I don't have when I'm working as an interpreter. It gave me a whole different perspective on how I do my job" (Selameab 2018, 2).

6.5 Of Race, Privilege, Power Dynamics, and (In)Visibility

Translation Studies scholar and literary translator Corine Tachtiris penned an opinion article titled "Privilege, Race, and Translation" in the June 2021 issue of *Words Without Borders*. Tachtiris starts with the premise that:

> [literary translators'] names are omitted from book covers, reviews, and promotional material as we wrangle over pennies per word and the

copyright to our own work. Given all that, it can be hard for some of us translators to think of ourselves as privileged. And yet White translators do generally benefit from privilege in various ways.

(Tachtiris 2021b)

She goes on to show that the scarcity of Black people and people of color (BIPOC) in the literary translation profession is highly problematic as their absence perpetuates a perceived inability to fulfill that role, and that translators of color face implicit and explicit biases in the publishing world (Tachtiris 2021b). The alleged unreliability of "native" interpreters and translators, whose fidelity could not be trusted, goes back centuries, as Tachtiris aptly shows, quoting Sir William Jones (1771 reprinted in 1969) referring to the risk incurred by the East India Company hiring native interpreters.

While Tachtiris scrutinizes the many systemic barriers for BIPOC, she also hits the nail on the head with a disturbing truth:

> The unacknowledged privileges of translating while White—being seen as qualified, being able to access resources that make the profession possible—can also predispose White translators to see themselves as the right person for a job.
>
> (Tachtiris 2021b, n. pag.)

Tachtiris's scholarship is focused on gender and race in translation, and her article was published at a time when the topic of race in translation was everywhere in the news, following the heated debate and controversy around the translators of Amanda Gorman's poem. Gorman, a then 22-year-old Black poet, read her poem "The Hill We Climb" at Joe Biden's presidential inauguration. "The Hill We Climb" became an instant success and foreign publishers rushed to find translators worldwide. However, the initially selected Dutch and Catalan translators created a heated controversy, because of whom they were, and not how they translated. Once again, theoretical reading and conceptual tools can be advantageously articulated to newspaper articles to help students reflect on a specific case. "Who translates what, for whom, and why do these questions matter?" can adequately be used as a starting point of a debate, a class presentation, or a story-telling project, to name but a few. Haidee Kotze's "Translation is the canary in the coalmine" (2021, n. pag.) poses essential questions about the visibility and invisibility of BIPOC in the literary translation arena and is a good addition to the "ethics in the news" reading section.

Issues of power and privileges can be addressed in multiple ways from a T&I ethics perspective. The mistrust and power differentials that Tachtiris (2021b) points out can also be observed in interpreted encounters, although more publications yet need to address how the interpreters' ethnic backgrounds influence how they are viewed in terms of their trustworthiness and ability to assert their authority and power as interpreters. Some useful readings to introduce the notion of power and interpreters as social beings in interpreted encounters include Mason and Ren's "Power in Face-to-Face Interpreting Events" (2012) and Fricklin and Jones's "Deciphering 'Voice' from 'Words': Interpreting Translation Practices in the Field" (2009).

Short exercises can be done in the online ethics classroom on the topics of race, gender, power, privilege, and visibility. They can take the form of discussion questions, classroom presentations, or storytelling, to name but a few. Questions can also be embedded in other assignments, such as in the reflective analysis of a videotaped interpreted encounter:

- Describe the protagonists in terms of social and professional backgrounds, ethnic and cultural backgrounds, and gender. How would you describe their respective powers in the encounter?
- Describe three of your own biases targeting specific groups of people and suggest ways of addressing these biases (this question was used in one of the authors' classroom and students were given a description of their instructor's own biases).
- Partner with another student whose LOTE is a language of lesser diffusion and, together, build a list of available resources for community interpreting in that LOTE.
- Assign a translation of a short text discussing white supremacy. This will encourage students to perform the closest reading of a text and engage with research on the topic.

A particularly useful reading for instructors interested in translating notions of race in the translation classroom is the compilation of resources put together by Tachtiris in a January 2021 *World Without Borders* article (Tachtiris 2021a). Despite more recent critiques challenging the origins of translation studies, as the one offered by Brian Baer in 2018 suggesting that the theorizing of the field actually started in Russian circles, when discussing issues of power, one cannot overlook the fact that T&I scholarship and educational frameworks have largely been produced in the West and are mostly Eurocentric (van Doorslaer 2011).

The authors hope that the newly created *Journal for Translation Studies in Africa*, whose first issue came out in May 2020, will address these urgent notions of power, authority, visibility and representativity from an African perspective. Marais and Delgado Luchner, the editors of the first issue, point out the urgency of introducing such issues in T&I training in Africa:

> [A]nyone who has researched translation phenomena on the African continent knows that language use in Africa is inherently political, much more so than in other parts of the globe. The historical events that have shaped current language policies and practices in Africa differ considerably from those that have led to the emergence of largely monolingual nation states in Europe. The coexistence of former colonial

languages, large vehicular languages and smaller local languages in the same geographic territory and the hierarchical distribution of language skills within African societies (where a high level of mastery of the colonial language is still often the privilege of the elites) makes translation between those different languages inherently asymmetrical and closely intertwined with existing power structures. Students who are not prepared to think about these aspects during their training might be ill prepared for the market.

(Marais and Delgado Luchner 2020, 2–3)

The ethics of representativity and visibility should also be considered from the makeup of T&I faculty members. How well are non-Western people represented among T&I instructors and what efforts are being made by institutions to stop perpetuating that disturbing model? Their absence contributes to what Tachtiris already pointed out, which is that BIPOC students have a harder time seeing themselves as the right person for a profession. This feeling is reinforced by the scarcity of BIPOC at T&I conferences and among board or leadership committees, a situation further reinforced by other invisible systemic barriers in T&I programs, which overwhelmingly offer powerful languages as language combinations.

6.6 Sample Assignments in the T&I Ethics Classroom

The sample assignments that follow are meant to raise students' awareness of the everyday ethical implications of their work as translators and/or interpreters. These implications transcend the codes of ethics and standards of practice drafted by T&I organizations, which should, of course, also be studied, analyzed, and discussed. Some of the topics selected for these T&I assignments are situated within the United States context (weapons, white supremacy speech, abortion, Native American people struggling to protect their land, to name but a few). Other assignments, such as the translation of a cigarette ad or of an excerpt from Hitler's *Mein Kampf*, used by one of the authors, have more "universal" topics and can be addressed by larger audiences.

6.6.1 Translation Assignment

"1 Watch the Introduction to Translation Assignments Video, which includes detailed information about defining one's audience.
 2 Translate the attached church pamphlet into your LOTE (language other than English). Pamphlet description: This is a church flyer posted online on the website of the Grace Baptist Church in New York State (USA). It is titled, 'Win a FREE AR-15.' The flyer is an invitation to a church assembly led by evangelist pastor and a NY assemblyman to talk about the right to bear arms with references to the Bible. The flyer

states that qualified attendees will receive a NY legally-modified AR-15 semi-automatic rifle.
3   Write a 400/500-word reflection addressing all the elements described. A sample translation reflection is provided in the Assignment folder. To be considered for a full grade, please refer to the rubric and follow all the instructions provided.

Before starting your translation, you should decide on a specific audience and the client who commissioned you for this assignment.

   a   Who is the end client?
   b   What is the purpose of this translation?
   c   Who is your imagined audience?

      • What country or group of countries are they from?
      • What is their socioeconomic profile and level of education?

   d   What is the potential impact of the interpreted content on yourself and your imagined audience?

4   Upload your 400/500-word reflection as a Word.doc here."

6.6.2 Interpretation Assignment

"**Interpret into your LOTE** (language other than English) the white nationalist speech by Richard Spencer and reflect on your performance and impact on yourself and on your target audience and culture.

Instructions for Your Interpretation Component:

1   Prior to recording your interpreting, look up any terminology you don't know in your LOTE and write down the possible translations.
2   For those who have never interpreted in a professional setting or are just starting out, consecutive interpreting is fine. If you already have experience interpreting and feel comfortable with it, try doing simultaneous interpreting. You can also play the video at a lower speed as needed.
3   Determine your recording device. This could be your phone, a digital recorder, software on your computer such as Audacity, etc., and set it up.
4   Play the video from the beginning using a headset, stopping every one or two complete thoughts (usually a complete thought is a sentence) if you are opting for consecutive interpreting. If you opted for simultaneous interpretation, instructions 5 to 9 do not apply to you. Just play the video with a headset and record your interpreted rendering without stopping.
5   Press record on your recording device, record your rendition of the one or two thoughts into your LOTE and pause the recording device.
6   Play another short segment of the recording.
7   Repeat step 5, recording your rendition into your LOTE.

8 Keep repeating this for the entire video.
9 Name your recording file adequately (see syllabus) to be considered for a full grade.
10 Upload your mp3 file of your interpreted rendition here.

Instructions for Your Reflection Component

Write a 400- to 500-word reflection addressing all the elements described. A sample translation reflection is provided in the Assignment folder. To be considered for a full grade, please refer to the rubric and follow all the instructions provided. Name your file according to the syllabus and upload your reflection as a Word.doc here.

The questions to address in your reflection include but are not limited to the following:

1 Who is the end client?

- A media outlet?
- An academic institution or NGO?
- A corporate company?
- Where are they based?

2 What is the intended purpose of the end client?
3 Who is your audience?

- What country or group of countries are they from?
- What is their socioeconomic profile and level of education?

4 What is the (possible) impact of the interpreted content on yourself and your imagined audience?"

6.7 Other Assignments for the Online Ethics Classroom

One of the authors, who started teaching an online ethics and standards of practice course in 2019, gradually moved away from longer or end-of-semester papers, as these did not seem to yield the expected results in terms of learning goals. Shorter assignments, including recorded presentations made available to the entire class on video documentaries (such as *Justice in Translation*, Blanco 2018) or movies (such as *Day One*, Hughes 2015, or *Un Traductor*, Barriuso and Barriuso 2018), along with a final class presentation analyzing ethical dilemmas within a selected case study, successfully replaced more traditional papers. The following assignment example is a new type of final project.

"**Purpose of Your Final Presentation:**

- **Demonstrate** your mastery of the codes of ethics and standards of practice covered in this course.
- **Showcase** your understanding of the course readings (15 readings pertaining to professional training, 8 readings pertaining to theoretical framework).

- **Demonstrate** your ability to articulate ethical dilemmas in a translation or interpreting scenario.
- **Apply** codes of ethics and standards of practice to ethical dilemmas (choose from the three codes of ethics analyzed in this course *and* any other code relevant to your case study).
- **Apply** core ideas from the course readings to your case study/dilemma situations.

Step One: Select a Case Study
  Use the following to identify case studies:

- Professional associations (websites, newsletters, etc.)
- The news
- Browser search in English and your LOTE
- Sample key words (not exhaustive):

'Ethical dilemma' + 'Interpreter'
  'Ethical issue' + 'Interpreter'
  'Moral dilemma' + 'Translator'
  Remember to:

- Include the US + other English-speaking countries (the UK, Australia, Canada, etc.).
- Increase your chances by looking for materials in your LOTE (Central/Latin America, Germany, China, Japan, Russia).

Make Sure Your Case Study is Sufficiently Complex
  Your case studies need to illustrate

- Hard-to-solve dilemmas
- Complex issues

Your case studies need to provide grounds for

- Elaborate discussions
- Subtle pros and cons

Your case studies need to be supported by

- Important concepts covered in the course
- References to/quotes from our course readings

Format of Your Presentations
  All presentations will be given live on [name of video conferencing tool] unless otherwise agreed upon with the instructor. Students unable to present live will reach out to their instructor to explain their individual situation.

Upon receiving permission to not present live, they will record their presentation and send it as an mp4 file to their instructor who will stream it during the live presentations.

- Each student will give a 10-minute oral presentation
  - Prepare about five to seven slides (flexible).
  - Make your presentation engaging: Do not prepare text-heavy slides that are intended to be read (use just a few words and images to trigger your audience) and do not read a scripted text.
  - Work on your public speaking skills.
  - Rehearse and time yourself.
- Other classmates will give feedback to each of their peers using the chat feature on [name of video conferencing tool]."

This type of final project was successfully experimented with in the spring of 2021. Adjustments for future iterations might include adding sufficient time for students listening to their peers to write their feedback in the chat, adding a break in the middle of the presentations, or scheduling two shorter sessions instead of a full half-day.

Additional ideas for assignments in the ethics classroom include, but are, of course, not limited to, the following:

- translation of a specific code of ethics from or into the language of instruction, accompanied by a reflection or a class presentation
- comparative analysis of codes of ethics from various countries (after asking students to read Sandra Hale's "Analyzing the Interpreter's Code of Ethics" (2007), for instance)
- critical analysis of codes of ethics and their shortcomings, including regarding the non-inclusion of translation and/or interpretation technology components as discussed earlier in this chapter
- critical analysis of an ethical principle across a selection of codes of ethics from various countries (after reading McDonough Dolmaya analyzing the definition of "accuracy" in her 2011's article titled "Moral ambiguity: Some shortcomings of professional codes of ethics for translators.")
- illustration of specific tenets of codes of ethics with practical situations in community settings, medical settings, or the courtroom
- creation of a code of ethics and standards of practice document for a community partner

Note

1 A detailed discussion on the topic of translation as a non-commodity, from a business perspective this time, can be framed with the American Translators Association's guide titled *Translation: Buying a non-commodity* (2008).

References

Acedo, Alicia Ruedo. "From the Classroom to the Job Market: Integrating Service-Learning and Community Translation in a Legal Translation Course." *Translating for the Community*, edited by Mustapha Taibi. Multilingual Matters, 2017, pp. 42–68.

Aguilar-Solano, Maria. "Non-Professional Volunteer Interpreting as an Institutionalized Practice in Healthcare: A Study on Interpreters' Personal Narratives." *The International Journal for Translation & Interpreting Research*, vol. 7, no. 3, 2015, pp. 132–48.

Albarino, Selma. "Facebook, Amazon, Twitter Research 'Blind Spot' in Modern Machine Translation." *Slator*, 19 July 2021, https://slator.com/facebook-amazon-twitter-research-blind-spot-in-modern-machine-translation/.

Baer, Brian James. "Teaching the History of Translation Studies." 2018, www.youtube.com/watch?v=Q6LboJLwTJs.

Baker, Mona. "Ethics in the Translation and Interpreting Curriculum." 15 Nov. 2015, www.monabaker.org/2015/11/15/ethics-in-the-translation-and-interpreting-curriculum/.

Barriuso, Rodrigo, and Stephan Barriuso. *Un Traductor*. 2018.

Bell, Chris. "Iranian Interpreter Defends Trump Speech Omissions." *BBC News*, 21 Sept. 2017, www.bbc.com/news/world-middle-east-41347217.

Bell, Terena. "Personal Ethics and Language Services." *Multilingual*, vol. 21, no. 8, 2010, pp. 41–3.

Blanco, Sergio. "La Palabra Justa/Justice in Translation." *The New York Times*, 2018, www.nytimes.com/interactive/2018/12/10/opinion/mexico-documentaries.html?emc=edit_na_20181211&nl=breaking-news&nlid=71394283ing-news&ref=headline.

Bowker, Lynne. "Translation Technology and Ethics." *The Routledge Handbook of Translation and Ethics*, edited by Kaisa Koskinen and N.K. Pokorn. Routledge, 2021, pp. 263–78.

Camayd-Freixas, Erik. "Statement to the Profession." *Proteus (Newsletter of the National Association of Judiciary Interpreters and Translators*, vol. 17, no. 3, 2008, www.najit.org/members_only/proteus/Proteus_Fall08w.pdf.

Camayd-Freixas, Erick. "Interpreting after the Largest ICE Raid in US History: A Personal Account." *Behind Bars: Latino/as and Prison in the United States*, edited by Suzanne Oboler. Palgrave Macmillan, 2009, pp. 159–73, https://cdn1.nyt.com/images/2008/07/14/opinion/14ed-camayd.pdf.

Chesterman, Andrew, and Emma Wagner. *Can Theory Help Translators? A Dialogue between the Ivory Tower and the Wordface*. Routledge, 2014.

Chew, Brandon. "Interpreters for Michigan Agencies Paid as Little as $4 per Hour." *Spartan News Room*, 5 Mar. 2021, https://news.jrn.msu.edu/2021/03/interpreters-for-michigan-agencies-paid-as-little-as-4-per-hour/.

Correa, Ellen, and Joseph Krupczynski. *Histories, Frameworks, and Approaches to Service Learning*. UMass Amherst Civic Engagement and Service Learning, 2019 2018.

Cote, Jackson. "Vanessa Marcotte Case: Language Expert Says Man Accused of Killing 27-Year-Old Woman Was given Poorly Translated DNA Consent Form." *MassLive*, 10 June 2021, www.masslive.com/worcester/2021/06/vanessa-marcotte-case-language-expert-says-man-accused-of-killing-27-year-old-woman-was-given-poorly-translated-dna-consent-form.html.

Crezee, Ineke. "Semi-Authentic Practices for Student Health Interpreters." *The International Journal for Translation & Interpreting Research*, vol. 7, no. 3, 2015, pp. 50–62.

Cronin, Michael. "Translation, Technology, and Climate Change." *The Routledge Handbook of Translation and Technology*, edited by Minako O'Hagan. Routledge, 2019.

Dolgon, Corey, et al. *The Cambridge Handbook of Service Learning and Community Engagement*, First paperback edition. Cambridge University Press, 2018, http://silk.library.umass.edu/login?url=https://search.ebscohost.com/login.aspx?direct=true&db=cat06087a&AN=umass.016949662&site=eds-live&scope=site.

Dolmaya, J.M. "Moral Ambiguity: Some Shortcomings of Professional Codes of Ethics for Translators." *Journal of Specialised Translation*, 2011, pp. 28–49.

Drugan, Joanna, and Rebecca Tipton. "Translation, Ethics, and Social Responsibility." *The Translator*, vol. 23, no. 2, 2017, pp. 119–25.

Elsen-Rooney, Michael. "NYC Investigation Department Mulls Probe into Language Interpretation Company after News Reports $4 Wages." *New York Daily News*, 25 Jan. 2021, www.nydailynews.com/new-york/ny-investigation-department-translation-probe-20210125-6uup3inm3newznzcnqmb5ciopi-story.html.

Faes, Florian. "Translate.Com Exposes Highly Sensitive Information in Massive Privacy Breach." *Slator*, 7 Sept. 2017.

Fricklin, L., and B. Jones. "Deciphering 'Voice' from 'Words': Interpreting Translation Practices in the Field." *Graduate Journal of Social Science*, vol. 6, no. 3, 2009, pp. 108–30.

"Fundamental Characteristics of a Profession." *Association of Public Policy Advocates of the European Union*, 10 Mar. 2016, www.aalep.eu/fundamental-characteristics-profession.

Hale, Sandra. "Analysing the Interpreter's Code of Ethics." *Community Interpreting*. Palgrave MacMillan, 2007, pp. 101–36.

The History of Service Learning. Los Angeles County Office of Education, www.lacoe.edu/portals/0/curriculum-instruction/slhistory_doc.pdf. Accessed 12 July 2021.

Hoza, J. "Toward an Interpreter Sensibility: Three Levels of Ethical Analysis and a Comprehensive Model of Ethical Decision-Making for Interpreters." *Journal of Interpretation*, 2003, pp. 1–48.

Hughes, Henry. *Day One*. AFI Conservatory, 2015.

Jones, William. *A Grammar of the Persian Language*. 1771. Scolar Press, 1969.

Kenny, Dorothy. "Technology and Translator Training." *The Routledge Handbook of Translation and Technology*, edited by Minako O'Hagan. Routledge, 2020.

Kenny, Dorothy, and Stephen Doherty. "Statistical Machine Translation in the Translation Curriculum: Overcoming Obstacles and Empowering Translators." *The Interpreter and Translator Trainer*, vol. 8, no. 2, 2014, pp. 276–94.

Kotze, Haidee. "Translation Is the Canary in the Coalmine." *Medium*, 15 Mar. 2021, https://haidee-kotze.medium.com/translation-is-the-canary-in-the-coalmine-c11c75a97660.

Love, Guthrun. "Sam Berner on the Ethics of Machine Translation." *Word for Word* (blog maintained by the New Zealand Society of Translators and Interpreters), 23 Jan. 2019, https://wordforwordonline.nzsti.org/2019/01/23/sam-berner-on-the-ethics-of-machine-translation/.

Marais, Kobus, and Carmen Delgado Luchner, eds. "Translation Studies in Africa: Quo Vadis." *Journal for Translation Studies in Africa*, vol. 1, 2020. Association for Translation Studies in Africa, https://journals.ufs.ac.za/index.php/jtsa/issue/view/434.

Mason, Ian, and Wen Ren. "Power in Face-to-Face Interpreting Events." *Translation and Interpreting Studies*, vol. 7, no. 2, 2012.

McDonough Dolmaya, Julie. "Moral Ambiguity: Some Shortcomings of Professional Codes of Ethics for Translators." *Jostrans*, vol. 11, 2011, www.jostrans.org/issue15/art_mcdonough.php.

Moorkens, Joss. "Under Pressure: Translation in Times of Austerity." *Perspectives*, vol. 25, no. 3, 2017, pp. 464–77.

Moorkens, Joss, and David Lewis. "Copyright and the Reuse of Translation as Data." *The Routledge Handbook of Translation and Technology*, edited by Minako O'Hagan. Routledge, 2020.

"NYC Mayor Requests LSP Investigation." *Multilingual*, Feb. 2021, https://multilingual.com/nyc-mayor-requests-linguistica-international-investigation/.

Perry, William. *Patterns of Development in Thought and Values of Students in Liberal Arts College: A Validation of a Scheme*. US Department of Health, Education and Welfare, 1968, https://files.eric.ed.gov/fulltext/ED024315.pdf.

Pilinu (user handle). "Some Ethics for MT Related to Endangered Languages." *Okchakko Translator Blog*, 24 May 2019, http://okchakko.com/blog/some-ethics-for-mt-related-to-endangered-languages/.

Preston, Julia. "An Interpreter Speaking Up for Migrants." *The New York Times*, 11 July 2008, www.nytimes.com/2008/07/11/us/11immig.html.

Quick, Karin, et al. "Creating and Evaluating Skills-Based Training in Working with Spoken-Language Interpreters for Oral Health Professions." *Journal of Dental Education*, vol. 83, no. 6, 2019, pp. 645–53.

Remen, Naomi. "Helping, Fixing, or Serving?" *Lion's Roar: Buddhist Wisdom for Our Time*, 6 Aug. 2017, www.lionsroar.com/helping-fixing-or-serving/.

Sarofian-Butin, Dan. "Me and the Devil Was Walkin' Side-by-Side: Demythologizing (and Reviewing) the Cambridge Handbook of Service Learning and Community Engagement." *Michigan Journal of Community Service Learning*, Fall 2017, pp. 165–71.

Selameab, Tehout. *Found in Translation: Key Findings from a Pilot Simulate-Based Training Experience for Interpreting and Oral Health Learners*. 2018.

Service-Learning Toolkit: A Guide for MSU Faculty and Instructors. Michigan State University, 2015, p. 132, https://communityengagedlearning.msu.edu/upload/toolkits/Service-Learning-Toolkit.pdf. Accessed 12 July 2021.

Tachtiris, Corine. "7 Resources on Translating Blackness, Race, and Racism." *Words Without Borders*, 8 Jan. 2021a.

Tachtiris, Corine. "Privilege, Race, and Translation." *Words Without Borders*, June 2021b, www.wordswithoutborders.org/article/june-2021-queer-privilege-race-and-translation-corine-tachtiris.

Taibi, Mustapha, and Uldis Ozolins. "Community Translation." *Bloomsbury*, 2016.

"Translation: Buying a Non-Commodity." *American Translators Association*, 2008.

van Doorslaer, Luc. "(More than) American Prisms on Eurocentrisms: An Interview Article." *Translation and Interpreting Studies*, vol. 6, no. 2, 2011, pp. 225–34.

Wadensjö, Cecilia. *Interpreting as Interaction*. Routledge, 1999.

Wang, Jun, et al. "Putting Words into the System's Mouth: A Targeted Attack on Neural Machine Translation Using Monolingual Data Poisoning." *Findings of the Association for Computational Linguistics: ACL-IJCNLP 2021*, Aug. 2021, pp. 1463–73.

Woll, Anne, et al. "Working with Interpreters as a Team in Health Care (WITH Care): Curriculum Tool Kit for Oral Health Professions." *MedEdPORTAL*, vol. 16, 2020, www.mededportal.org/doi/full/10.15766/mep_2374-8265.10894.

7 Conclusion
Final Considerations

The term accessibility is at the heart of everything we propose in this book, and as such, we believe it is important that good education is made available to all students, with diverse educational, linguistic, and cultural backgrounds. Differently from most countries around the world, the United States, where both authors are situated and teach, has a very specific T&I education structure, where higher education is more readily available at the graduate and postgraduate levels, with very few T&I undergraduate (bachelor's) programs available to students. Moreover, most T&I programs are language-specific. This situation creates a landscape where the teaching of community translation and interpreting, for example, apart from a few exceptions, is relegated to for-profit short workshops, employers' short training modules, and 2-year technical schools, which further divides our field. Therefore, we did not set out to suggest pedagogical frameworks only for graduate and postgraduate courses and programs. Rather, we hope that our ideas and concepts for online translation and interpreting education can be used by all instructors and curriculum designers in different scenarios, including undergraduate initiatives and shorter training workshops to meet the increasing demands for trained translators and interpreters in all areas of society.

We have shared ideas on different types of assignments, assessments, and rubrics for a range of T&I educators: Those who have never taught translation and interpreting online before (both synchronous and asynchronous) as well as those who are experienced instructors or have had some level of exposure to remote teaching as a result of the COVID-19 world pandemic. In doing so, one additional goal has also been to challenge long-standing notions about how translation and interpreting should be taught (e.g., the mother-tongue principle) and to propose new pedagogical frameworks with online learning as our main focus, but which can definitely be adapted for in-person interactions as well. However, as we pen these lines, many reports have already been issued suggesting that remote learning is likely to last even after the pandemic is over. School district administrators in the United States want "to offer students more flexibility, meeting parent or student demand, meeting the diversity of students' needs, and maintaining

DOI: 10.4324/9781003149316-8

student enrollment" (Schwartz et al. 2020). Such plans are not only being made by primary and secondary educational leaders. In "Beyond COVID-19: What's Next for Teaching and Learning in Higher Education," John Nworie reminds institutions and educators that the lessons learned from the emergency pivot to remote education during this global public health crisis should not be discarded, but that "effort, and innovative resources will be required in order to improve on these gains and make them sustainable" (2021, n.pg.). Everything indicates that this new modality of engaging with education is here to stay.

At the same time, the pandemic has also revealed enormous gaps and inequities among learners and their access to technology,

> not all students will have access to regular internet service, or top-of-the-line software and hardware. . . . Students may have unstable, unpredictable, or generally low levels of access to the internet or to WiFi; they may rely on data plans which may run low or run out before they have completed all their coursework; they may lack access to physical devices like laptops, tablets, printers, webcams, or other equipment; they may not have access to specialized software; or they may be unable to run certain apps or software on their devices. Though there may be community-based resources to address some of these access issues (e.g., free WiFi at public libraries and coffee shops), these resources may not be accessible to all students when they need them, or may not be available at all in the event of community-level closures.
>
> (Jungels 2020, n. pag.)

Government agencies, institutions, educational leaders, and instructors must find ways to address such challenges and disparities. At the level of instruction, we have included several ideas in the book to make content more accessible and offer different options for students' participation in class (written, oral, and video comments, and file attachments). Asynchronous activities tend to be more flexible, for instance, in that students have different days and times to add their contributions, thus having opportunities to submit work when their Internet connection is stronger and faster. Moreover, a great idea to find out more about our students and their concerns and issues with accessing resources before the online course begins is to ask them! This can be done by using different online survey platforms, document sharing apps such as Google Docs, or even via email.

We stressed many times throughout the book that educators and trainers should be prepared to dedicate a lot of time to the design phase of an online course. In addition to developing engaging content, instructors must be constantly checking and double-checking instructions, links, assignment submission dates, and activities. A suggestion is to ask the instructional design team of one's institution to review courses before they go live, or, in the spirit of collaboration and co-construction of best practices, asking for peer feedback from other instructors or program directors. To keep themselves abreast of the latest developments and tools, online educators should attend remote learning conferences and consider taking remote courses themselves—stepping into the shoes of distant learners provides an invaluable perspective to future remote instructors. Moreover, as always, instructors should have plans B, C, D, and so on and so forth, since the level of unpredictability with technology cannot be underestimated.

As far as teaching the course itself, instructors are advised to carefully weigh time-consuming activities (i.e., facilitating an online debate can take many hours). Therefore, as suggested, trusting students to be in charge of a weekly discussion, and randomly checking students' discussion comments, as opposed to reading every single comment, is one way to address the issue. We also propose to humbly accept not to be perfect at all times: Accepting small glitches in lecture videos (as discussed in Chapter 4), showing one's imperfection, and embracing some vulnerability adds humanity to our teaching. We invite educators to apply some of the tenets of the pedagogy of vulnerability, in which a more collaborative form of teaching is created (Brantmeier 2013). In this framework, students and teachers are sharing, learning from each other, and embarking together on a journey of discovery, with "an approach to education that invites vulnerability and deepened learning through a process of self and mutual disclosure on the part of co-learners in the classroom. The premise is simple—share, co-learn, and admit you don't know" (3).

Similar to educators, students must also be prepared to engage with education in a different way and with a distinct mindset. Learners need to be or become even more independent and self-regulated than in in-person experiences, so that they "*take ownership of learning* as much as [instructors] are creating the conditions conducive to translator competence" (Washbourne 2013, 377). Moreover, many of the face-to-face educational norms that students are familiar with do not apply to online courses and students first need to become aware of online modalities. They should take advantage of all the resources provided by their institutions, or, for courses not attached to universities or colleges, online course developers. Sometimes, instructors themselves must take charge of providing additional support, which can be in the form of tutorials or Q&As, or even dedicate the first module of the online class to "learning how to navigate your online course."

We reiterate that the syllabi designed for an online environment should be extremely detailed, which is all the more true for fully asynchronous courses. For instance, we proposed incorporating a clickable table of contents in the form of FAQ to help students immediately locate the answer to their questions. It is helpful to draft these FAQs from the perspective of the students and use the first person "I" ("What if I have technical issues?"). This approach anticipates the types of questions that students would typically ask in a classroom and is more inviting. Anticipation and iteration are crucial components of any successful online course. Instructors should repeat elements of the syllabus in the LMS course shell and vice-versa, establishing bridges between these two instruments.

Studies show that the selection of a learning management system, while most of the time outside of the purview of instructors, weighs heavily on the students' learning experiences. Some LMSs have been designed with an instructivist framework in mind and need to be supplemented with collaborative tools to allow students to actively participate in their own learning process, interact with each other, co-construct meaning, and benefit from each other's challenges and successes. Indeed, one of the trickiest challenges of teaching and learning online is the risk of isolation, both on the instructors' and students' sides. Implementing tools and spaces for interaction and establishing one's presence is key. As we pointed out in Chapter 4, establishing instructor online presence is not exactly a science. Rather, it is akin to an art, based on one's willingness to experiment with new ideas. In asynchronous classes, instructors will convey their personal tone and approach to teaching via a variety of written, audio, or video communication channels. While cognitive and teaching presence are usually not an issue, social presence is sometimes the one component that is missing in online courses. Establishing one's social presence can take many forms, yet at least needs to include a form of validation, which can be addressed to the entire group, highlighting specific achievements, sharing snippets from their weekly reflections, or any other form of validation. Asking students permission to use their anonymized work as an exemplar is another form of validation. Such items can not only serve as learning objects (McGreal 2004) in future iterations of a given course, but can, if properly introduced as student-generated learning objects, also serve modeling goals for future students. These small actions go a long way in establishing one's presence and reiterating the "I see you, I hear you, I respond to you" and "I validate you" sentiments that are so crucial to establishing student engagement.

One thing is yet undisputable: The timeliness and frequency of instructor-student communications are key elements in asynchronous settings. Detailed and timely comments and evaluations allow students to learn from their mistakes and apply guidance in terms of research skills, methodology, and critical thinking to their next assignment. Best practices in feedback encourage instructors to strive for balance between corrective feedback and encouragement or praise. Yet it is unfortunate that feedback is still too often associated with fault-finding, as feedback should be a means to reinforce learning in a positive way, which means acknowledging progress, newly implemented skills, creativity, and progression toward professionalism, for instance.

If teaching a semester-long course, the first two weeks of classes should be envisioned as crucial to setting expectations, encouraging students to review the syllabus and guiding them through the course content on the LMS, identifying the needs of a new cohort, and having individual online meetings with students who need them. These face-to-face meetings also allow students to see their instructor as a "real" human being. It is important that instructors envision each of these early exchanges with students as an opportunity to reinforce expectations and encourage them to review the syllabus, online resources, and tutorials. As a matter of fact, recent studies suggest that bichronous courses, mixing synchronous and asynchronous elements, are linked to higher retention rates and are conducive to student success (Martin et al. 2020; Farros et al. 2020).

We highlight the importance of educators designing clear learning outcomes for their T&I courses, which should always be aligned with assessments. The guiding question when writing course goals and objectives should always be, "what will students be able to do at the end of this class?" Moreover, when considering ways to measure students' knowledge and skills, instructors should develop a clear understanding of the different learning process levels, such as the ones proposed many years ago by pedagogue Benjamin Bloom, and revised for the online environment by Andrew Churches in 2008, as follows:

- remembering
- understanding
- applying
- analyzing
- evaluating
- creating

Of course, rubrics play an important role in assessing the aforementioned levels of learning as they set out educators' expectations regarding the quality level of students' engagements with various assignments. They also provide students with a roadmap for self-assessment, a key component of reflective practice. We have shared several examples of scoring tools for translation and interpreting exercises, which can be used or adapted by any instructor based on their own course objectives and goals.

In the last chapter, we argue that ethics should be at the core of online T&I curricula and not only taught in a designated ethics course, but should be included, in one form or another, in any T&I class. Since ethical questions are multifaceted and part of any translator's and interpreter's life, students need to be equipped with theoretical concepts, prepared for deep critical thinking, and able to bridge theoretical concepts with everyday ethical dilemmas, those happening in their professional life and those heard on the news. Students should engage with a variety of codes of ethics and standards of practice, be encouraged to discuss and compare these codes, and challenge specific tenets, weighing contexts, audiences, and outcomes. As Baker points out "ethical decisions must be *situated*" (2015, n. pag.). Some insufficiently addressed ethics topics include machine translation (Bowker 2021) and translation technology in general (Bowker 2021; Cronin

2019), as well as the livelihood and working conditions of translators and interpreters around the world (Moorkens 2017).

We suggest in the same section that issues of power, privilege, and visibility should also be included in the T&I classroom ("Who translates what, for whom, and why do these questions matter?") and that these notions extend to the makeup of T&I faculty members. The absence of people of color and underrepresented people contributes to what Tachtiris (2021b) exposed, which is that non-Western students have a harder time seeing themselves as the right person for a profession.

We would be remiss not to address the topic of high-maintenance students, which can be closely tied to their lack of self-regulation skills. In face-to-face courses, brief conversations before or after class are very helpful for discussing lower grades, lack of progress, misunderstandings, or any other topic causing disappointment to students. In remote education, early intervention is key: Instructors need to identify and address these issues immediately. Emails are not the right medium for these exchanges, instead, we strongly advise turning to short teleconference meetings. Electronic communications, however, can be used to document and summarize what was said during the meeting.

Last but not least, remember to take care of yourself. Online teaching "requires balancing a lot of competing needs and expectations—a balancing act that can be stressful and require more emotional labor than usual" (Jungels 2020). As mentioned previously, allowing yourself to be vulnerable and transparent with your students goes a long way in dealing with issues that might happen. Actually, it is not that issues might happen; they will! Moreover, the same way you assist your students when they are struggling, remember to ask for help from people you work with, other instructors, university or program leadership, as well as friends and family.

References

Baker, Mona. "Ethics in the Translation and Interpreting Curriculum." 15 Nov. 2015, www.monabaker.org/2015/11/15/ethics-in-the-translation-and-interpreting-curriculum/.

Bowker, Lynne. "Translation Technology and Ethics." *The Routledge Handbook of Translation and Ethics*, edited by Kaisa Koskinen and N.K. Pokorn. Routledge, 2021, pp. 263–78.

Brantmeier, E.J. "Pedagogy of Vulnerability: Definitions, Assumptions, and Applications." *Re-Envisioning Higher Education: Embodied Pathways to Wisdom and Transformation.*, edited by J. Lin et al. Information Age Publishing, 2013, https://blogit.jamk.fi/tecsummerschool/files/2013/05/Ed-Brantmeier-Pedagogy-of-Vulnerability-Definitions-Assumptions-Applications.pdf.

Churches, Andrew. "Bloom's Digital Taxonomy." 2008, https://www.academia.edu/30868755/Andrew_Churches_Blooms_Digital_Taxonomy_pdf.

Cronin, Michael. "Translation, Technology, and Climate Change." *The Routledge Handbook of Translation and Technology*, edited by Minako O'Hagan. Routledge, 2019.

Farros, Jesslyn Nicole, et al. "Online Learning: The Effect of Synchronous Discussion Sessions in Asynchronous Courses." *Journal of Behavioral Education*, November 2020.

Jungels, Amanda. "Inclusion, Equity, and Access While Teaching Remotely." *Rice University: Center for Teaching Excellence*, 13 Mar. 2020, https://cte.rice.edu/blogarchive/2020/3/13/inclusion-equity-and-access-while-teaching-remotely.

Martin, Florence, et al. "Bichronous Online Learning: Blending Asynchronous and Synchronous Online Learning." *Educause Review*, 8 Sept. 2020, https://er.educause.edu/articles/2020/9/bichronous-online-learning-blending-asynchronous-and-synchronous-online-learning.

McGreal, Rory. *Online Education Using Learning Objects*. Routledge/Falmer, 2004.

Moorkens, Joss. "Under Pressure: Translation in Times of Austerity." *Perspectives*, vol. 25, no. 3, 2017, pp. 464–77.

Nworie, John. "Beyond COVID-19: What's Next for Online Teaching and Learning in Higher Education?" *Educause Review*, 19 May 2021, https://er.educause.edu/articles/2021/5/beyond-covid-19-whats-next-for-online-teaching-and-learning-in-higher-education.

Schwartz, Heather L., et al. "Remote Learning Is Here to Stay: Results from the First American School District Panel." *Rand Corporation*, 2020, www.rand.org/pubs/research_reports/RRA956-1.html.

Tachtiris, Corine. "Privilege, Race, and Translation." *Words Without Borders*, June 2021, www.wordswithoutborders.org/article/june-2021-queer-privilege-race-and-translation-corine-tachtiris.

Washbourne, Richard Kelly. "The Self-Directed Learner: Intentionality in Translator Training and Education." *Perspective Studies in Translatology*, vol. 22, no. 3, Oct. 2013, pp. 373–87.

Index

abduction, induction, and deduction 30
accessibility 19, 21, 26, 53, 59, 71, 143
Acedo, Alicia Ruedo 126, 129
aesthetic-usability effect 72
Afolabi, Segun 15
Aguilar-Solano, Maria 121
Albarino, Selma 124
Alim, H. Samy 19
Allen, I. Elaine 15
Aloni, Nimrod 6
Altman, Jane 92
Anderson, Lorin W. 54, 67, 68
Anderson, Terry 67, 86, 87
Angelelli, Claudia 42
Archer, Walter 67, 68
assessments 2, 24–25, 33, 49, 54–55, 85–89, 97, 125, 143, 147; formative assessments 87; summative assessments 87
assignments 4, 6, 15, 21–22, 24–25, 31, 41, 45, 48–52, 54–56, 60–61, 63–64, 66–67, 70, 72, 75–82, 85, 87, 89, 92–93, 97–99, 101–103, 115, 118–120, 124, 127–129, 133–136, 138, 143–144, 146–147
asynchronous 16, 21–23, 37, 41, 49, 50, 63, 68–69, 76, 82, 85, 92, 124, 143–147
Azizinezhad, Masoud 16

Badalotti, Floriana 96
Baer, Brian James 133
Baker, Mona 116, 119, 121, 122, 147
Barnacle, Robyn 1
Barnett, Ronald 1
Barrett, Frank J. 11
Barriuso, Rodrigo 136

Barriuso, Stephan 136
Barros Filho, Eduardo A. 15
Bartlomiejczyk, Magdalena 89
Basamalah, Salah 7
Baxter, Baril 58
Bednarski, Betty 5, 2
Bell, Chris 120
Bell, Terena 118
Berg, Richard 59
bichronous learning 68–69, 147
Bilić, Viktorija 16
Blanco, Sergio 136
Blinne, Kristen C. 49
Bloom's taxonomy 54, 87, 92; Bloom's Digital Taxonomy 88
Bond, Esther 16
Bowker, Lynne 122, 123, 124, 147
Brantmeier, E.J. 145

Camayd-Freixas, Erik 117
Campbell, S. 48
CAT tools 31, 60, 75–76, 88, 123
Chan, Kai 44
Chen, Nian-Shing 16
Chernov, Ghelly V. 92
Chesterman, Andrew 85, 115
Chew, Brandon 120
Choi, Jung Yoon 89
Churches, Andrew 88, 147
Clifford, James 5
codes of ethics 94, 117–118, 120, 123, 134, 136–138, 147
Colina, Sonia 42
community of inquiry (CoI) 22, 67, 68
computer assisted interpreting (CAI) 27
connectivism 63
Cormier, Dave 4
Correa, Ellen 126

Costa, Karen 70, 71, 72, 73, 74
Costa, Vonessa 64
Cote, Jackson 120
Crezee, Ineke 129
Cronin, Michael 124, 147
Culturally Responsive Pedagogy 19–20

Dall'Albaa, Gloria 1
Darby, Flower 15, 49
Deleuze, Gilles 10
Delgado Luchner, Carmen 133, 134
deliberate practice 10, 32, 34, 76
Demmans Epp, C. 55, 56
Dewey, John 2
diagnostic tests 86
digital literacies 64, 65
Dimitrova Englund, Birgitta 30
Doherty, Stephen 124
Dolgon, Corey 126
Dolmaya, J.M. 123, 138
Drugan, Joanna 119

Ehrensberger-Dow, Maureen 8
Elsen-Rooney, Michael 120
engagement 73, 85, 93–95, 97, 116, 125–126, 146; student engagement 21, 23–24, 49, 50
Ericsson, K. Anders 34
ethical dilemmas 118, 120, 136, 137, 147

Fadiman, Anne 44
Faes, Florian 122
Family Education Rights and Privacy Act (FERPA) 18
Fantinuoli, Claudio 27
Farros, Jesslyn Nicole 68, 147
Fowler, Rachel C. 68
Fricklin, L. 133

Garrison, D.R 68, 68
Gile, Daniel 92
González-Davies, María 5, 43, 44
Gorozhanov, Alexey I. 16
Guatarri, Félix 10
Guo, Philip J. 59
Guseynova, Innara A. 16

Hale, Sandra 138
Hashemi, Masoud 16
Heinberg, R. 71
Herring, Rachel 34
Hlavac, Jim 20

Hollenbeck, John 54, 55
Horton, William K. 2
Hoza, J. 119
Hughes, Henry 136

instructor feedback 40, 76

Jafar, Afshan 49
Jay-Rayon Ibrahim Aibo, Laurence 11, 33, 45, 69, 100
Jones, B. 133
Jones, William 132
Jungels, Amanda 144, 148
Jun Pan, Yang 1

Kelly, Rob 59
Kenny, Dorothy 124
Kiraly, Don 34
Ko, Leong 16
Kosichenko, Elena F. 16
Koskinen, Kaisa 8
Kotze, Haidee 132
Krathwohl, David 54
Krupczynski, Joseph 126
Kuto, Emmanuel Kobena 96

Ladson-Billings, Gloria 19
Langdon, Elena 69, 100
language reviewers 103, 106–107, 111–113
languages of lesser diffusion (LDD) 20, 43, 112
languages of wider diffusion 43, 44, 45
learning management system (LMS) 16, 24–25, 35, 39, 42, 49, 52–53, 55–56, 58, 60–61, 66–67, 82, 86, 93, 97, 146
learning outcomes 8, 25, 54–55, 67–68, 86–88, 101, 147
lecture videos 71–72, 75, 145; pre-recorded videos 71, 82
Lederer, Marianne 92
Levinas, Emmanuel 5
Lewis, David 123
Love, Guthrun 122
Lynch, Laura 26

machine interpreting (MI) 27
machine translation (MT) 7, 26–27, 50, 116, 122, 124, 147
Marais, Kobus 133, 134
Martin, Florence 147
Mason, Ian 94, 133

Massey, Gary 8
massive open online courses (MOOCs) 18
Mazzei, Cristiano 11, 33, 38, 69, 70, 100
McGreal, Rory 70, 146
McTighe, Jay 35
minority languages 44, 112
Misfeldt, Morten 2
modeling 32, 36, 70, 73, 119, 146; modeling, scaffolding, and reflection 32
Moorkens, Joss 120, 123, 148
Moser-Mercer, Barbara 31
mother tongue principle 96, 143
Motta, M. 32
multilingual courses 16, 44, 59, 78, 82, 85, 98, 107
Muñoz Martín 8
Musampa, Emmanuel Kambaja 96

new-traditional students 70
Nilson, L. B. 33
Nworie, John 144

online education 14–15, 18–19, 27, 35, 67, 83
Oyetoyan, Oludamilola I. 15
Ozolins, Uldis 43

Paris, Django 19
Parr, Tony 96
peer feedback 76, 80, 82, 86, 145
Perramon, María 16
Pilinu 122
Pokorn, N.K. 96
power 10, 15, 20, 35, 44, 58, 71, 73, 128, 130–134, 148; powerful languages 44, 134
presence: cognitive presence 67–68; online presence 63, 67, 69, 146; social presence 22, 60, 67–68, 70, 146; teaching presence 67–68, 70, 73, 75
Preston, Julia 117
process-oriented 40, 50, 76, 97
Pym, Anthony 3

Quick, Karin 130

race 132–133
Reefer, Kayla 16

reflection 31–32, 36–37, 39, 41–42, 48, 67, 97–100, 126, 135–136, 158; reflective practice 24, 32, 34–35, 41, 76, 99, 147; self-reflection 4, 11, 47, 76–77
Remen, Naomi 128
remote interpreting (RI) 23, 27, 64, 106, 131
remote simultaneous interpreting (RSI) 60
Ren, Wen 94, 133
Rendón, Laura 70, 71
Resnick, M. 2
Robinson, Douglas 30, 31
rubrics 7, 37, 39, 41, 48, 51, 73, 76, 90, 92–93, 97–104, 106–108, 135–136

Sabah, Salman Sabbah 50
Sachtleben, Annette 16
safe practice 48, 98, 129
Sarofian-Butin, Dan 126
scaffolding 2, 32, 98
Schunk, D.H. 33
Schwartz, Heather L. 144
Seaman, Jeff 15
Seaman, Julia E. 15
Selameab, Tehout 131
Seleskovitch, Danica 92
self-directed learner 47
self-evaluation 48, 49, 70
sentipensante pedagogy 71
Serres, Michel 1
service-learning 116, 122, 125–129
Shaffer, David Williamson 2
situated 1, 115, 119, 126, 130, 134, 143, 147
Skov Fougt, Simon 2
socio-constructivism 63, 76
Suojanen, Tytti 8
synchronous 14, 16, 21–23, 37, 59, 63, 68–70, 75–76, 82–83, 87, 92, 103, 124, 143, 147

Tachtiris, Corine 131–134, 148
Taibi, Mustapha 43, 128, 138
Thormann, Joan 4
Tipton, Rebecca 119
Tuominen, Tiina 8
Tymoczko, Maria 43

Ugarte, Xus 16
Universal Design for Learning (UDL) 20

video capture (screen-recorders) 54, 55, 58, 59
VoiceThread 23, 25, 35, 42, 51, 56, 58, 60–61, 63, 69, 83, 92, 94, 98–99, 120
volunteering 116, 122
volunteerism 121–122, 125

Wadensjö, Cecilia 130
Wagner, Emma 85
Wang, Honghua 1
Wang, Jun 124
Washbourne, Richard Kelly 1, 47, 48, 76, 77, 145

Weiss, Mike 19
Whitehead, Alfred North 2
Whitmer, J. 56
Wiggins, Grant P. 35
Woll, Anne 130

Xiu Yan, Jackie 1

Yamagata-Lynch, Lisa C. 68
Yee, Megan 48

Zhao, Guoping 5
Zimmerman, B.J. 33
Zimmerman, Isa Kaftal 4

Printed in the United States
by Baker & Taylor Publisher Services